Contents

List of illustrations

Colour plates

Acknowledgements

Douglas Sutherland and Jack Chance would like to express their thanks to Mr Vare and Mr Cockburn-Mercer of Hardy Bros. Ltd, Mr Woodcock of C. Farlow & Co. Ltd and Mr Muirhead of John Dickson & Son for supplying many of the flies used to illustrate this book.

Credits

All the colour photography is by Gavin Cottrell. The black and white photographs on pages 36, 68, 84, 96, 108 and 118 are reproduced by permission of John Marchington and the illustration on page 16 by permission of BBC Hulton Picture Library. The hook sizes on page 130 are reproduced by permission of O. Mustad and Sön, Norway.

The diagram on page 57 and the other drawings in this book are by Charlie Sutherland.

Foreword

LORD BIDDULPH

I should start by saying that it is a considerable privilege to have been asked to put pen to paper to write the foreword to this extremely interesting and unique book. Surely there must be amongst the thousands, if not hundreds of thousands of freshwater fly fishermen many others who would be far better qualified than I to perform this pleasant task, not only as far more proficient anglers but as writers as well.

I think I know how it all came about. Some time ago Douglas Sutherland's brother and I were engaged in an abortive attempt to try to catch eels on a famous river system in the Western Isles of Scotland. There were the usual number of salmon anglers staying at the lodge and there were a considerable number of grilse around at the time, so I fished for salmon and the author's brother, John, fished for eels only occasionally accompanied by myself, I not caring very much for the horrible slippery things! Anyhow, it transpired that I had better luck than he did and after a few days' fishing my score had reached thirty-six salmon.

Those who read this can be assured that this splendid catch was not attributable to any particular skills that I might have as an angler, but rather to the fact that there were a lot of salmon around and I just happened to be in the right place at the right time (surely in any fishing good luck is half the game), namely fishing the River Grimersta on the Isle of Lewis. One can only presume therefore that the news spread around and eventually reached the author that here was an experienced and skilful angler, who obviously knew everything about flies and what fly to use on the appropriate occasion.

I can assure everyone that this is not so at all. Every time I open my fly box and gaze at the assorted array of brightly coloured fur and feathers, a feeling of gloom pervades me. I wonder if anyone else has had the same feeling; nothing in the box looks right at all and one is convinced that all the flies in the box are useless and precious time is going to be wasted flogging the water with something that no self-respecting fish would dream of looking at or, at the very best, probably only just rise to turn away disgusted with the offering. And we all know how often that can happen!

Surely this book has just got to help, and I am truly delighted that it has been written and so beautifully illustrated. Now when selecting a fly I shall do so with much greater confidence, armed with the knowledge written by real experts.

It is, I suppose, true to say that if I have any claim to fame at all it lies in the fact that I have fished all my life. To be on a river bank with a fly rod in my hand and preferably a few salmon around to catch, is without doubt for me the most pleasant situation possible. I have also fished a great many lakes, loch, rivers, streams, and some reservoirs throughout the British Isles. I have fished in Europe and Iceland and Ireland. Fishing must be in the blood; one is either a fisherman or not. I can look back to my very early youth and the thrill of catching minnows in a jar in the clear chalk streams of Hampshire, goldfish on a bent pin baited with bread attached to a piece of string attached to the end of a bamboo pole and now, the real thrill for me is the rise and take of a salmon to the carefully chosen fly.

All the flies tied by all the fly tyers around the world will not be of much use if there are no fish to catch. I suppose the continued plentiful existence of the brown and rainbow trout is reasonably well assured because both are fairly easy to rear in captivity and release. It is, in my opinion, the salmon and sea trout, and particularly the Atlantic salmon, whose survival, because of man's greed, is in real danger. If we could assure the salmon 1) an adequate breeding stock, 2) a suitable environment to live in and 3) sufficient food for the juvenile fish during their early life in the rivers, and plentiful supplies of feeding during their life in the sea, there would perhaps be no problem. But all this is liable to be wasted when one looks at the problems confronting the future of the salmon. These are:

Pollution including the effects of acid rain:
Afforestation and drainage causing the erosion of the spawning beds and gravel:
Predators, the worst of which is possibly *Helichoerus Grypus*, grey seal, over whose sleek head so much controversy rages:
Industrial fishing at sea done mainly by the Greenlanders and Faroese with Ireland and Norway and even the United Kingdom running close behind them:

And lastly, but by no means least significant, poaching and the use of monofilament hang and drifting gill nets.

It always seems odd to me that there is legislation to protect the salmon once it has arrived back at its river of origin (although some would question whether this legislation is as effective as it might be), but little or no legislation to protect it once it goes to the sea to feed and grow. There is legislation to control the fishing of whales, herring, cod, and suchlike, and frenzied argument about the culling of seals, but what about the poor salmon who spends about half his life in the sea? It will not be until we establish adequate international laws, and review existing legislation, and establish appropriate organisations with the requisite authority to achieve these aims and the necessary muscle to enforce the law, that the future of *salmo salar* will look brighter.

Well, I've been at the fishing game quite a long time now, and they say the older the dog the wiser. But when I come to look at it I really am none the wiser as to why salmon take a fly at all when they don't feed in fresh water, and why a trout will take a particular fly on a particular day and not look at it on another.

Perhaps some of the answers are in this book, but then again, much of the joy of fishing is the element of uncertainty. The real experts are the first to admit that they do not know all the answers. For my part, long may the mysteries of fishing and fish remain unsolved. It is the very uncertainty of the game that makes the triumph sweeter and the blank days easier to be philosophical about.

There is only one thing I know for certain: 'Ye'll ne'er catch a fush unless your flea is in the watter!' as we say in Scotland.

What fly and when? Well now, in this delightful book I am sure that we will have been given at least some of the answers.

Introduction

DOUGLAS SUTHERLAND

Amongst the many dicta attributed to Samuel Johnson, Hawker, in his *Instructions to Young Sportsmen* quotes the revered doctor as opining:

'Fly fishing may be a very pleasant amusement; but angling or float fishing I can only compare to a stick and a string, with a worm at one end and a fool at the other.'

That the great lexiographer appears to believe that fly fishing is not angling or vice versa would not have worried him. When asked by an earnest seeker after truth why he had defined a 'pastern' in his famous dictionary as the 'knee' of a horse, Johnson replied with the utmost good humour: 'Ignorance, madam. Pure ignorance.'

Anglers, down the ages, would not so readily forgive him for suggesting that fishing with the fly is in any way superior, either in effectiveness or in the pleasure other methods afford to their devotees.

Almost exactly a hundred years earlier a rather more respected authority had written:

'Angling may be said to be so like mathematics that it can be never learnt.'

Who would not wholeheartedly agree with that most complete of all anglers, Izaak Walton?

Walton was not only catholic-minded in the variety of fish he pursued but willing to experiment with any bait from a fly to a live frog.

Nowadays we tend to live in the age of the specialist who forswears any other form than that which he regards as the highest form of the angler's art.

The art of using a frog as a lure may nowadays be on the decline. On the other hand, there must be many, like myself, who have been addicted to fishing from early boyhood and whose earliest successes were with a worm cunningly impaled on a hook.

Even today, to come home with a good basket of trout, after a day fishing a Highland burn, upstream in low water with a worm, gives me a warm glow of satisfaction that my early skills have not entirely deserted me.

The definition of an angler is clear. It is one who sets out to catch his fish with rod, line and hook. How the hook is presented, be it disguised however simply or elaborately, the definition sets it aside from any other kind of fishing.

This book is devoted to fishing flies. Not, let it be noted, to fly fishing, which is quite a different matter. Should the reader who has perused these pages thus far believe that after careful study of the pages which follow he will *overnight* become the hero of the riverbank, a giant in the eyes of his fellow practitioners of the gentle art, I must urge him to return this book immediately to the bookshop or library shelf where he chanced upon it.

Even the emphasis that this book is about fishing flies requires qualification.

When the book was first discussed with the publishers, I was quite properly asked to define as exactly as possible what it was hoped to achieve which had not already been covered in a field in which so much had already been written.

It was not an easy question. Was this book to be a dictionary or even a compendium with the inference that in its pages would be found every fly which had ever been offered to trout or salmon? Obviously not. To attempt this would be to court disaster.

I can well remember a learned friend who had assisted in the compilation of the *Concise Oxford Dictionary* complaining bitterly that an irate customer had demanded his money back on the grounds that he had bought the work to look up the meaning of some particularly abstruse word and failed to find it.

Imagine, therefore, the opprobrium which my collaborator Jack Chance and I would incur were we to make any encyclopaedic claims for this book. There must be few devoted fly fishermen who do not have some secret weapon tucked away in a corner of their fly box. The more secret the more indignant they might be at its omission; such is the perversity of human nature.

On the other hand, we have been at some pains to ensure that the flies here illustrated will be widely representative.

We are conscious also that of all the types of lure designed to catch fish, the fly is uniquely an art form in itself. There are a great and increasing number of fly fishermen who get almost as much pleasure in tying their own flies as they do in casting them upon the water. Indeed, some of the most expert tiers of flies find the art to be an end in itself and leave it to others to demonstrate their effectiveness.

I have remarked that this book is primarily a book about fishing flies and not about fly fishing. This is true. At the same time, the book would be of much less worth were it not for the contribution of the distinguished team of experts who have been enlisted to write each section.

I would venture to assert that there is no fisherman in the land who would claim to write with authority on every aspect of fly fishing, from casting for the lordly salmon to the delicate skills of nymphing for trout or the comparatively new technique of reservoir fishing.

It is for this reason that we have asked acknowledged experts in each branch of the fly fisher's art to give the reader the benefit of their own, highly personalised views of their own art form.

That we have been able to assemble such a galaxy of talent, Jack Chance and I must count as a proud achievement. Rather than make the customary perfunctory acknowledgement of our gratitude to them in this introduction, we have prefaced each of their contributions with a brief biographical sketch.

I have said that this book will not make the newcomer the hero of the riverbank overnight, but it is our sincere hope that it will at least put us all in with a better chance!

Salmon flies of
Great Britain

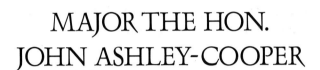

MAJOR THE HON.
JOHN ASHLEY-COOPER

John Ashley-Cooper, like all the contributors to this book, has been a fisherman all his life.

During World War II he saw service in the Middle East and since demobilisation his main interest in life has been fishing and particularly fishing for salmon. Salmon fishing is a subject on which he is an acknowledged expert and one is tempted to venture the opinion that he has possibly caught more salmon than any other person alive today.

His home is in Wimborne in Dorset and he is a member of the Fisheries Advisory Committee of the Wessex Water Authority and a former Secretary of the Test and Itchen Fishing Association as well as being a director of the old-established firm of Farlow and Company known to fishermen throughout the world.

John Ashley-Cooper has fished extensively for salmon in Scotland, England, Ireland, Norway and Iceland, where shortly after the war he built a fishing lodge. In 1980 the publishing firm of Victor Gollancz brought out his much acclaimed work, Great Salmon Rivers of Scotland.

Evolution and development

The story is a long one. The earliest written mention of a salmon fly in Britain is to be found in the *Book of St Albans*, under the section headed *Treatyse of Fishing with an Angle*, compiled by Dame Juliana Berners, Prioress of Sopwell, and printed at St Albans in 1496. How extensive was the real knowledge of this learned lady about salmon flies is open to doubt; nevertheless there it is – after recommending 'worms and a sovereign bait that breedeth on a waterdock' as suitable lures for salmon, Dame Juliana continues: 'Also, ye may take him with a dubbe (i.e. fly) at such times when he leapeth, in like form and manner as ye do take a trout and grayling . . .', direct evidence to the modern protagonists of floating lines and carbon graphite rods (if it is any comfort to them) that the origin of their art goes back at least to the era of the Wars of the Roses, if not earlier!

17

Thomas Barker in *The Art of Angling* (1657) says: 'If you angle for him with a fly (which he will rise at like a trout) the fly must be made of a large hook, which hook must carry six wings, or four at least. There is judgement in making up of these flies.' Barker also has the first recipe for dressing a salmon fly. He further caught a salmon in the Thames with the aid of his new-fangled 'winch', and he also used a 'landing hook' (the first recorded mention of a gaff). Before this date the salmon fisherman's line had always been made fast to the tip of the rod. It was of plaited horsehair and up to twenty-six yards in length, of fifteen or more plies of hair. If any modern salmon fisherman feels that he lacks entertainment, it might be interesting to attempt playing a lively fifteen-pounder on a home-made outfit of this description!

Richard Franck and Robert Venables were both noted salmon fishers of the mid-seventeenth century. Both, curiously enough, were Cromwellian soldiers, whose tour of duty took them to Scotland and Ireland respectively; this doubtless gave them ample opportunity to practise their sport, and later to write about it. Franck's *Northern Memoirs*, published in 1658, has copious instructions for the making of salmon flies, and for their use in many different Scottish rivers as far north as Ross-shire.

Down the years such notable writers as Robert Venables in his *Experienced Angler* or *Angling Improved* (1662) and James Chetham in his *Angler's Vade Mecum* (1681) wrote in detail about the use and construction of salmon flies.

The *North Country Angler* (1786) gives the dressing of a double-winged salmon fly, and the *Driffield Angler* (1808) describes Macintosh's Black Dog (amongst six other dressings) as follows:

Wings: Bluish feather from a heron wing, with spotted reddish turkey tail feather.
Body: Lead coloured pig's wool.
Throat and hackle: Large black cock's hackle.
Head: Dark green mohair.

Would such a dressing, in spite of its longevity, not be perfectly effective for killing salmon in these modern days? Incidentally, Macintosh mentions that he caught a salmon of fifty-four-and-a-half pounds at Castle Menzies (on the Tay near Aberfeldy) on a fly in 1765. It is the large weight of this fish rather than the fact that it was caught on a fly which is brought into prominence in his story. This would seem to indicate that fly fishing in Scotland at that date was a common enough practice.

One other interesting dressing of this period may be noted. It is that

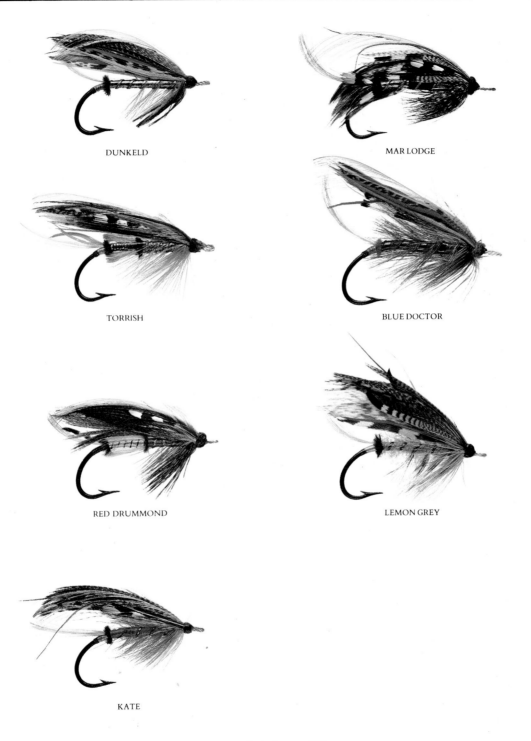

DUNKELD

MAR LODGE

TORRISH

BLUE DOCTOR

RED DRUMMOND

LEMON GREY

KATE

Gut-eyed Salmon Flies

of the oldest salmon fly still in existence which, at least until recently, as recorded in the Lonsdale Library volume on Salmon Fishing, was still in the possession of Messrs Allcock and Company, the well-known tackle makers. This actual fly was thought to have been dressed in 1775 and is made up as follows:

Wings: Peacock tail covert.
Throat: Dark blue dun cock.
Body: Pig's wool and mohair, dyed orange and red and undyed.
Tag: Silver tinsel (flat).
Head: Peacock herl.

Would this dressing too not be perfectly effective nowadays?

It should also be remembered that until about 1835 all salmon flies were dressed with the end of the line, whether of plaited horsehair sometimes mixed with silk, or later of gut, whipped to the shank of the hook. William Scrope in *Days and Nights of Salmon Fishing* described Duncan Grant's tackle, on which he caught the fifty-four pound salmon at Wester Elchies on the Spey, as having 'thirty plies of hair next the fly'. This should have given a strong breaking strain, of approaching thirty pounds. This episode took place in the early 1800s.

The older generation of present day fishers may remember the trout flies of their youth being sometimes whipped to short lengths of gut in a similar way. It was a bad system, and had obvious weaknesses; nevertheless gut-eyed flies, which could be detached at will from the cast, were not invented or in general use till about 1835 or after.

Nineteenth-century development to the stage of the fully-dressed built-wing fly

The nineteenth century saw a greatly increased literary output on salmon flies and fly fishing generally, with no lack either of illustrations of popular patterns, or of actual flies that have survived into modern times. So there is a wealth of evidence as to the way in which salmon flies developed during this period.

What is more, it was in this century that salmon fishing became firmly established as a sport rather than as the mere killing of fish. Fly fishing became *de rigueur* as a sporting method, bait fishing being only tolerated towards the end of the century in certain waters, and even then being considered a somewhat underhand practice.

The construction of railways also contributed indirectly towards the development of salmon flies. Railways spreading all over the country

20

from 1830 onwards meant a much wider scope of activity for salmon anglers, who consequently proliferated in numbers, and demanded a widely increased range of flies, both in pattern and quantity. The nineteenth century inventor and tyer of salmon flies was thus encouraged to give full vent to his creative imagination.

We are well familiar with the form and appearance of salmon flies in the early nineteenth century, if only from coloured illustrations such as that of four flies given by G. C. Bainbridge in his *Fly Fishers' Guide* (1816). The hooks look somewhat unsound, but the dressings would be perfectly serviceable if copied today.

In 1828 Sir Humphry Davy wrote an excellent book *Salmonia*, mainly about salmon fishing in the Scottish Highlands. He said that the best salmon flies had dun and brown bodies, with silver ribbing, red and black hackle, and wings of kingfisher and golden pheasant. The best hooks were made by O'Shaughnessy of Limerick, while London hooks were apt to bend or break. In many ways Sir Humphry Davy was ahead of his age. He realised that salmon 'did not willingly load themselves with food', and their stomachs when opened were always found to be empty. When they took food they were influenced by dim memories of parr-hood. This was highly advanced thinking at that time; even by the end of the century many fishermen still refused to believe that salmon did not feed in fresh water!

It seems that by the 1830s, and possibly earlier, different styles of fly dressing and different local patterns had developed on most of the principal British salmon rivers. For instance there were Tweed flies, as described by Scrope in 1843, namely Kinmont Willie, The Lady of Mertoun, Toppy, Michael Scott, Meg with the Muckle Mouth, and Meg in her Braws. A. E. Knox in 1872 lists 'old' Spey flies such as Gold and Silver Speal, Gold and Silver Reeach, Green Black and Purple King, Gold and Black Heron, and the Carron Fly amongst others. The Tay had its Black Dog and other rivers had their particular favourites.

These old types of salmon fly all tended to be of sombre colour, and made of easily obtainable local materials – but in the 1840s a new metamorphosis took place.

At Limerick in Ireland during the early part of the century there had arisen a new style of fly dressing, employing in addition to golden pheasant the most exotic types of tropical feathers, such as blue and green parrot, blue, red and yellow hackle points, scarlet ibis, blue macaw, summer duck and Indian crow, amongst others. All these, when combined with dyed swan and floss silks of every vivid colour, served to

LOGIE

SILVER GREY

BLUE CHARM

SIR RICHARD

LADY CAROLINE

Gut-eyed Salmon Flies

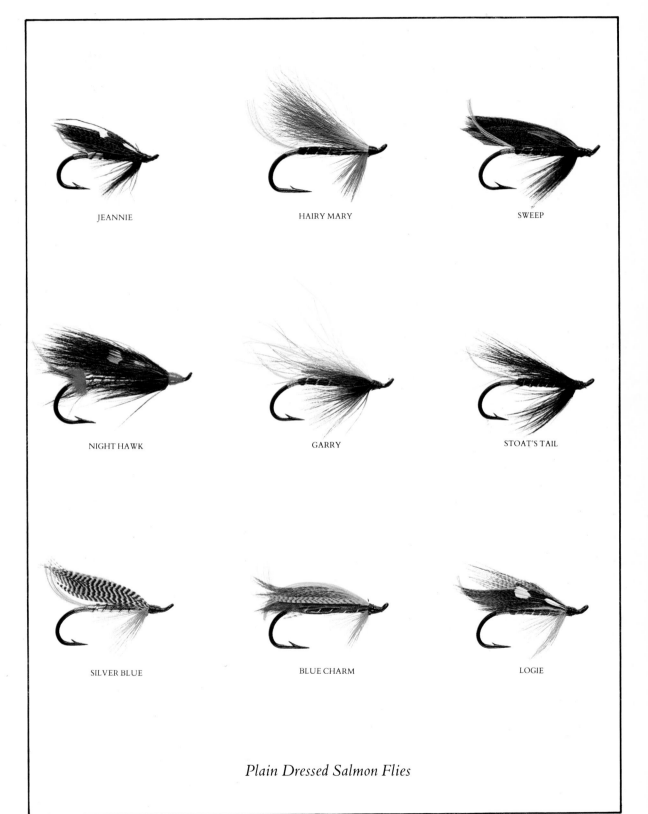

JEANNIE

HAIRY MARY

SWEEP

NIGHT HAWK

GARRY

STOAT'S TAIL

SILVER BLUE

BLUE CHARM

LOGIE

Plain Dressed Salmon Flies

produce flies of brilliantly striking hues and character, which to the human eye at least appeared outstandingly attractive. The two most famous Irish fly designers were O'Gorman and Rogan of Ballyshannon.

When introduced from Ireland into the rest of Britain, flies dressed in this manner soon bid fair to oust in popularity the older types of traditional local fly. Thus one saw the advent of such elaborate patterns as the Black Goldfinch, Lee Blue, Lemon Grey, Popham, and Sir Richard to give but a few examples.

For the most part the introduction of this new and spectacular type of dressing prevailed. Though more sombre local patterns such as the Black Heron, Green or Purple King, Akroyd, Dallas, Glentana, March Brown, Lady Caroline and others of similar type did survive, they were vastly outshone in numbers as well as in outward show by the huge variety of intricately tied built wing patterns based on the imported Irish style of dressing. Such dressings, no doubt because they took the human fancy, were supposed to be more attractive to salmon.

It is interesting that it has taken a hundred years or more for the wheel to turn full circle. Nowadays the tendency is back towards simplicity in flies once again, in design, colour and construction, for example Stoat's Tail, Black Tosh, Garry Dog, Hairy Mary, Munro's Killer, etc.

At this point some mention should be made of the famous fly tyer of Sprouston, James Wright, who flourished in the middle years of the nineteenth century. Sprouston is on the south bank of the Tweed three miles downstream from Kelso; and Wright was responsible for the original of so many of the different popular flies that we are apt to take for granted. For instance the Silver Grey, Durham Ranger, Thunder and Lightning, Silver Black and Blue Doctor, Dandy and White Wing, as well as others, all owe their origin to this master of his craft.

Thus we see by stages the development of the fully dressed Victorian salmon fly in all its splendour of tip, tag, tail, butt, body, body ribbing, veils, body hackle, throat hackle, under-wing, over-wing, topping, horns, cheeks, and head. Patterns of fly were endless. Francis Francis in his *Book on Angling* in 1867 gives two hundred and thirty-five patterns, all involving elaborate tying. Different patterns were assigned with great care to different rivers all over Britain. Traherne in the Badminton Library *Salmon and Trout* (1887) gives only twenty-one well-known patterns, but Kelson in *The Salmon Fly* (1895) gives two hundred and fifty. Most of the well-known favourites appear amongst these, though there were many others as well. One need only mention as representatives the Jock Scott, Dusty Miller, Silver Grey, Silver Doctor, Mar Lodge, Blue Charm, Gordon, Logie, Akroyd, Torrish, Thunder and Lightning, and Jeannie.

In fact, by the end of the nineteenth century the cult of the fully dressed salmon fly had reached its zenith, and there was little room for development in this field.

At this stage it was still not generally accepted amongst anglers that salmon did not feed in fresh water (although certain keen observers had noted that the salmon's stomach when he was caught was invariably empty), but what form of food a salmon fly represented was left in doubt (as indeed is still the case, though to a lesser extent). Perhaps no one really cared, but it was often thought that changes of fly pattern would induce a fish to take, in the same way as in trout fishing. Scrope, for example, in *Days and Nights of Salmon Fishing* avows: 'Concerning these flies I will note one thing, which is, that if you rise a fish with the Lady of Mertoun, and he does not touch her, give him a rest and come over him with the Toppy, and you have him to a certainty, and *vice versa*. This I hold to be an invaluable secret, and is the only change that in my long practice I have found eminently successful.'

Traherne too in the Badminton Library *Salmon and Trout* assures us: 'The Silver Grey makes a capital change with the Lion – the two most valued silver bodied flies in general use.' How much value was there in such changes? Let modern salmon fly fishermen form their own estimate.' And how much value is to be found at any time in changes of pattern alone, perhaps from a Logie to a Blue Charm of the same size, or from a Silver Grey to a Thunder and Lightning, and so on?

And how much value did special patterns of fly provide on different rivers? For instance was it really an advantage to use a Gordon on the Dee, or Silver Wilkinson on the Tweed, a Bulldog on the Eden, a Lemon Grey on the Cork Blackwater, or a Black Dog on the Tay? Many Victorian fishermen would definitely have said so, but maybe this was purely a figment of their imagination.

One thing of great benefit was, however, coming into general use at the end of the nineteenth century, and that was the metal eye on the salmon fly hook, as opposed to the gut eye which quickly rotted. The early metal eyes were apparently clumsy and many of the pundits such as Kelson, were to start with very much against them. But this invention was too valuable to be overridden; and as metal eyes improved in design they quickly, and rightly, became a *sine qua non* in all future flies, both for salmon and trout.

GREEN HIGHLANDER

SILVER DOCTOR

DUSTY MILLER

THUNDER & LIGHTNING

JOCK SCOTT

HAIRY MARY

Moose Hair Salmon Flies

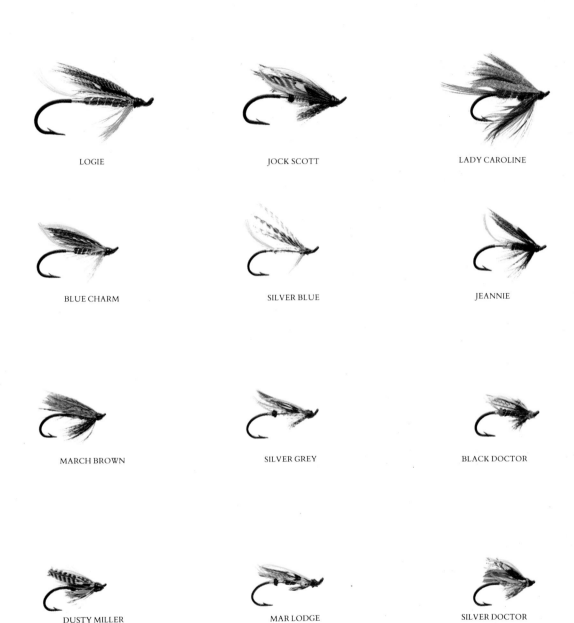

LOGIE   JOCK SCOTT   LADY CAROLINE

BLUE CHARM   SILVER BLUE   JEANNIE

MARCH BROWN   SILVER GREY   BLACK DOCTOR

DUSTY MILLER   MAR LODGE   SILVER DOCTOR

Low Water Salmon Flies

Double hooks for flies had also been introduced in Victorian times, both in large and small sizes, as an alternative to single hooks.

The development of the salmon fly in the twentieth century

The early 1900s saw little change in the design of flies or the theories governing their use. Crosfield and Chaytor were great tyers of the period. The former tied elaborately, trying to make each feather component play its part, and the latter simply, in revolt against elaborate Victorian dressings. The flies of both achieved reasonable success but not in any outstandingly marked manner.

Mr A. H. Wood of Cairnton in the 1920s showed that Dee salmon in low clear water preferred remarkably small and thinly dressed flies fished near the surface. His special long-shanked fine wire hooks have however since been shown to be too liable to tear out of a hooked fish's mouth in strong currents and big rivers. These hooks, although still used, are no longer generally popular.

Apart from greater emphasis on 'streamlining' and 'modified' thinner dressing, fly design in fact saw no revolutionary change until after the Second World War, when hair-wing flies started to come into general popularity. This was something both new and effective. The earliest hair-wing fly was probably the Garry Dog, first produced on the Tweed in the 1920s, the inventor using the hairs from the tail of his dog, Garry and naming the fly accordingly. After 1945 other hair-wing flies began to make their appearance. The Hairy Mary came from Inverness, the Stoat's Tail from Park on the Dee, and the Black Tosh, again named by its inventor E. Ritchie after his collie dog which supplied the hair, from Delfur on the Spey. Hair-wing flies could be tied on single, double or treble hooks, or on light, or heavy tubes as required. They were especially useful on tubes in the large sizes with their hair wing up to three and a half or even four inches long, for use with an appropriately sized treble hook, so much better a hooker and holder than the old 6/0 to 8/0 single or double hooks.

All the above patterns had marked success and they have lately been followed by a swarm of similar ones with variations only in the length and colour of hair, or colour of hackle and body. Salmon appear to be largely open-minded to all shades of colour, and only to take notice of length and bulk, apart from motion. In cold water long hair is best, also often in fast water whether warm or cold. In clear water the hair should be thinly dressed, in coloured water more thickly. As the water becomes warmer the length of the hair should be proportionately reduced, until in the 60s°F. fish will often take very small Stoat's Tails or similar sparse dressings.

What a change from the days of Kelson, when if a built-wing lacked a topping or a jungle cock cheek, it might well be discarded as being no longer fit for duty! Nowadays it has been shown that simple black hair is more attractive to Atlantic salmon anywhere than all the ornamentation which to human eyes at any rate made the Victorian fly a complete work of art. How are the mighty fallen! Hair wings now have gone far to oust feather wings, though the simpler patterns of the latter may still be found frequently in use, for example, the Blue Charm, Logie, Black Heron, Lady Caroline, Thunder and Lightning, March Brown, Silver Blue, Fiery Brown and Jeannie amongst others, but the large sized built-wing feather flies have virtually disappeared from the fly box.

All that is required of the hair wing is that it should be of the appropriate length and texture (fairly fine so that each hair can vibrate in the water, giving a markedly lifelike illusion), also of the desired colour, whether black (which is as good as anything), or dyed yellow or orange for use in coloured water, or a mixture of these or of other colours.

As to the elaborate hackles, bodies, and tails of the flies of bygone days, all have been shown up as largely unnecessary, except in the simplest forms. Black hair by itself on a hook or tube will catch fish as well or even better than anything else, and will look more lifelike, besides which it is more durable and is far cheaper, quicker, and easier to tie.

Dry flies

I have made no mention so far of dry flies for salmon in Britain. The reason is that dry fly fishing has never had more than a very limited success this side of the Atlantic, and for that reason is seldom used here. It is true that salmon have occasionally been caught on a mayfly on rivers such as the Test, or on dry flies on other rivers elsewhere, but such cases are a rarity. No doubt the obvious is true that more fish would be caught on dry fly if it was more used! But one feels that, when conditions are such that British salmon could be caught on a dry fly, they could probably be caught much more easily by a more orthodox method. Also, in contrast to what happens in Canada, it should be remembered that the majority of fresh run British fish enter our rivers when the water is fairly cold or at least under 60°F. in temperature. Does the use of a dry fly need warmer water, coupled with the presence of fresh fish, to be

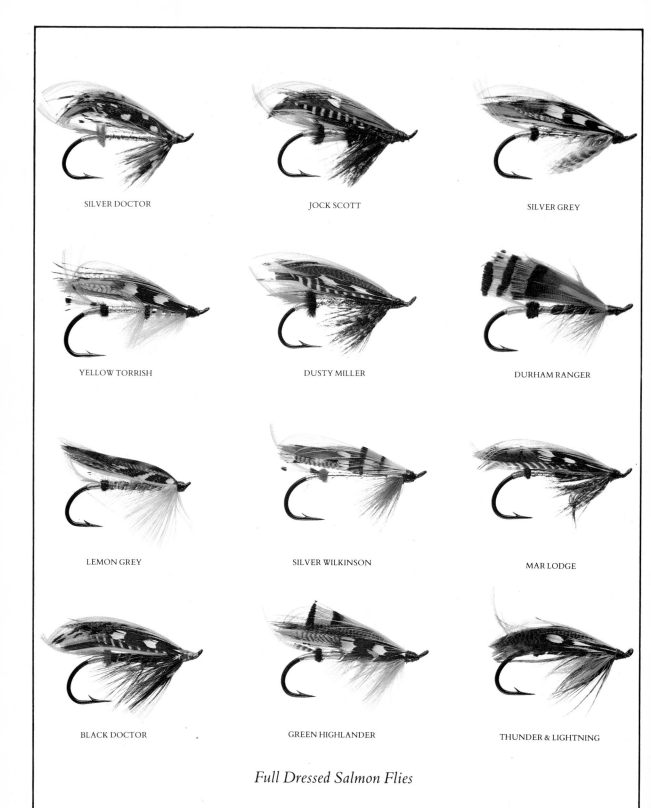

SILVER DOCTOR

JOCK SCOTT

SILVER GREY

YELLOW TORRISH

DUSTY MILLER

DURHAM RANGER

LEMON GREY

SILVER WILKINSON

MAR LODGE

BLACK DOCTOR

GREEN HIGHLANDER

THUNDER & LIGHTNING

Full Dressed Salmon Flies

ESMOND DRURY –
THUNDER & LIGHTNING

GOLD & BLUE VARIANT

ESMOND DRURY –
SILVER DOCTOR

ESMOND DRURY –
HAIRY MARY

GENERAL PRACTITIONER

SHRIMP

ESMOND DRURY –
TORRISH

BLUE ELVER

ESMOND DRURY –
STOAT'S TAIL

ESMOND DRURY –
SHRIMP

ESMOND DRURY –
BLUE CHARM

ESMOND DRURY –
JEANNIE

Salmon Flies of Great Britain

reasonably successful? Canadian experience rather suggests this.

In any case, any dry flies used here would probably be of the American patterns, such as the Pink Lady, White or Grey Wulff, Rat-Faced McDougall, or Quill Gordon. There are no traditional British dry flies for salmon.

The history of certain well-known salmon flies

JOCK SCOTT

This is perhaps the best known salmon fly of all time and it has probably killed more fish than any other.

John or 'Jock' Scott, who invented this fly, was fisherman to Lord John Scott on the Tweed in the 1840s. In 1845, during a voyage to Norway, Jock devised this dressing, which proved a successful one. In subsequent years Jock was employed as fly dresser to Mr Forrest, the tackle maker at Kelso. One day the fisherman at Bemersyde came into the shop and invited Mr Forrest up for a day's fishing. The latter did well with Jock's fly and caught three salmon. He was so pleased that he christened the fly after its maker and so it has remained ever since.

It was with a Jock Scott that General Home killed a fifty-one-and-a-half pounder on the Tweed in 1921. Many other fish of note have been killed on it.

SILVER WILKINSON

This in former years was a very popular Tweed fly, and for a long time no Tweed boatman would look at any other pattern. It was invented in 1859 by the Rev. P. S. Wilkinson for use on the Tweed. He originally named this fly the Silver Belle, and it was only later that its name was changed. Messrs Farlow still have the original fly in their pattern book. It was on a 4/0 Silver Wilkinson that Mr Pryor caught the record Tweed salmon of fifty-seven-and-a-half pounds at Floors in 1886, and Mr Brereton caught a fifty-five-pounder on a 'small' Wilkinson at Mertoun in 1889.

LADY CAROLINE

This fly is named after Lady Caroline Gordon Lennox, daughter of the Duke of Richmond and Gordon of Gordon Castle on the Spey in the last century. It is an old Spey dressing, described by Sir Herbert Maxwell in 1913 as 'a fly of very ancient type, named after a lady still with us'. The Lady Caroline is still popular and is frequently used nowadays.

DURHAM RANGER

This well-known fly was an invention of James Wright, the famous fly tyer of Sprouston on the Tweed in the mid-nineteenth century. The story went that a party of English fishermen came up from Durham to fish the Tweed and Wright devised this fly for them. It was successful and was appropriately christened the 'Durham Ranger'. It is a showy fly, with its golden pheasant tipper wing, and is useful in high or coloured water, being one of the fully dressed Victorian patterns still in periodic use today.

THUNDER AND LIGHTNING

Another pattern invented by James Wright of Sprouston in the mid-nineteenth century. This has always been a popular dressing and still is so at the present day. Kelson in 1895 describes it as 'exceedingly popular, and has a well-earned reputation for its destructive qualities at a time when rivers begin to rise after rain'.

The dressing is a comparatively simple one, but the brown mallard wing, the orange and blue jay hackles, and the black body with its gold ribbing are in pleasing contrast. It is as good a feather-winged fly for clear water as can be found anywhere.

AKROYD

A Dee strip-wing fly invented by Mr Charles Akroyd of Brora about 1880. The 'strip-wing' flies had the peculiar feature of wings made of cinnamon or alternatively white strips of turkey feather, tied close to the body in 'penthouse' fashion and separated. The jungle cock cheeks were tied in sloping downwards and alongside the throat hackles. Long heron hackles and a thin silver ribbed floss silk body completed the ensemble.

The Akroyd has been found a killing clear water pattern, and is still sometimes used. Other similar 'strip wing' dressings are the Glentana, the Tartan, and the Jock O'Dee.

Conclusion

It is hoped that the above brief history of the evolution and development of the British salmon fly to its modern stage may prove of some interest. As to the future, who is to say? Any improvement on the best of modern patterns would seem difficult to attain. Perhaps if the sea food of the salmon could be identified and classified with more certainty, further progress in the imitative design of flies might result. It is sad in any case to think that those beautiful works of art such as Jock Scotts, Dusty Millers,

Durham Rangers, Wilkinsons, and Pophams, belonging to an earlier age, will soon be museum pieces; but that appears to be the trend of the moment. Let us hope that the salmon flies of the future, even if inevitably less attractive to the human eye, will compensate by providing an ever-increasing allure to the fish.

Sea trout flies

HUGH FALKUS

Hugh Falkus has probably fished for and caught a greater variety of fish than anyone else writing on the subject today but it is as a fisherman for sea trout that he is probably best known in the piscatorial world.

Once a Spitfire pilot in the Battle of Britain, he was shot down over France and his almost miraculous escape from death is beautifully described in his book of memoirs The Stolen Years.

Hugh Falkus is, however, much more of an all-round sportsman than he is normally given credit for. He is, of course, a distinguished writer, a naturalist and a film director and broadcaster whose work for the B.B.C's Natural History Unit has achieved for him international acclaim. He was responsible for such B.B.C. TV classics as Salmo the Leaper *and, more recently,* Highland Story. *There was also a film made about his own home life, called appropriately* Self Portrait of a Happy Man.

He won the 1969 Italia Prize for his film Signals for Survival, *a documentary about animal communication, which also achieved the American Blue Ribbon of 1971. He has recently been granted the Royal Geographical Society's Cherry Kearton Medal and Award for his writing and films on wildlife.*

His book about animal behaviour, Nature Detective, *was a best seller and his book* Sea Trout Fishing *has become a classic.*

Before discussing sea trout flies it would be sensible to take a glance at the fish itself.

The sea trout is a migratory brown trout, although there its likeness to the brown trout ends. It is similar in appearance to the salmon, but has very different habits. And right at the start it is necessary to appreciate that sea trout fly fishing is neither a branch of brown trout nor of salmon fishing, it is a sport entirely of its own.

Unlike the brown trout and to a lesser degree the salmon, about both of which history has much to relate, the sea trout is a very 'recent' fish. Until a comparatively short time ago almost nothing was known about it. Even as recently as 1916, in his book *The Sea Trout, A Study in Natural History*, Henry Lamond asks: 'What is a sea trout?' And continues:

> 'It is, one must admit, a question which has not yet been very satisfactorily answered by anybody, nor can I pretend to give a very satisfactory answer myself.'

In fact, Lamond wrote a very well-informed and intelligent book, which includes a highly significant observation. Referring to the voracious feeding of young sea trout in salt water before their return to the river, he says:

> 'There is good reason, beyond the mere growth of the fish for this extreme voracity, because the sea trout has now to lay up within its tissues a reserve of energy-making fat sufficient to meet not only the exhausting journey to the upper waters, but the more exhaustive process of the development of the milt and ova.'

In other words, Lamond had realised something that, to the angler, is of the utmost importance: *the sea trout's ability to fast in fresh water while waiting to spawn.*

The slowness of some anglers to appreciate the significance of this was reflected in their approach to sea trout fishing, which resulted in the sport becoming hedged by convention and occasional absurdities. For instance, fifty years ago (when I was a boy, and can well remember) fly fishing 'purists', failing to distinguish between brown trout and sea trout behaviour, and thinking that the canons of brown trout fishing should apply equally to sea trout, regarded people using the Alexandra as being quite beyond the pale! R. C. Bridgett refers to it in his book *Sea Trout Fishing* (1929):

> 'The Alexandra, the mere mention of which in certain company is enough to call forth a storm of protest and is liable to give the innocent offender the reputation of being an arrant poacher, is an excellent tail fly in Connemara. It was responsible for the taking of some heavy fish and could secure a victim whenever one was required to cheer a hardworking, unrewarded rod about to lose hope. Some unthinking people, deceived by the silver body and by the manner in which the wing-material lies over the hook, declare the Alexandra to be nothing more or less than a minnow, and advocate its expulsion from a fly water, whereas a minnow equal in size to a No. 10 Limerick is a transparent creature, almost invisible to human eye and not at all silvery. Brown trout know a minnow when they see it, but what living creature they or sea trout mistake an Alexandra for, I do not know.'

Nor did anybody else. And nor does it matter. The Alexandra is, quite simply, a flashy sort of lure. And none the worse for that. Like salmon flies, most of the flies used for sea trout fishing are, simply, lures. Few of them, after all, are imitations intended to deceive a feeding fish.

It is highly unlikely that a migratory fish, carrying its rations on its back and having no need of food, takes a fly because it is hungry. Almost certainly it has lost its appetite on its return to fresh water and, when it 'takes' most probably does so from force of habit: the feeding habit it has indulged during its recent life at sea and during its earlier life in the river as a parr.

But this was not the popular concept. According to legend, migratory fish continued to feed on their return from sea; a view that earlier angling writers had done nothing to discourage (and in the following passage sea trout are included with salmon, since in those days no distinction was made between them).

> 'For Salmon being Fish of Prey, and great Feeders, Nature directs them to the salt Waters, as Physick to purge and cleanse them, not only from their Impurities after Spawning, but from all their muddy terrene Particles and gross Humours, acquired by their extraordinary, excessive Feeding all the Summer in fresh Rivers . . . And when they are fatted and glutted with their long, excessive Feeding in Fresh Rivers, and have spawned in the latter end of the Year, repair to the Sea for Warmness, and to be purged from the gross Humours by the Calidity of the Saline Water; and when Winter is over, return to their Summer Habitations.'

So wrote Robert Howlett in *The Angler's Sure Guide* (1706). And this misconception has lasted for a long time. Even today, reluctant to believe that migratory fish can survive so long a period without food, many people are suspicious of the salmon's abstinence and remain convinced that returning sea trout feed as avidly in fresh water as in the sea.

That such a belief should persist into modern times is strange. Quite apart from the observation of sea trout behaviour and examination of their stomach contents after capture, a little thought puts the matter beyond doubt. And a detailed analysis of this will be found worthwhile, for it has a considerable bearing on our fly fishing strategy.

Like salmon, the huge numbers of sea trout that run into fresh water each year eat very little for the good reason that there is very little for them to eat. Most of our waters hold only a small proportion of the food that would be necessary to support such vast populations of migratory fish with normal appetites, in addition, of course, to the populations of resident species.

While in salt water (as I have seen for myself) sea trout feed greedily. If they retained their appetites and continued to hunt as actively in fresh water, we might expect that the longer they remained in this new and less

A selection of traditional dapping flies of fifty to sixty years ago, many of which are from Loch Maree

*A selection of traditional dapping flies of fifty to sixty
years ago, many of which are from Loch Maree*

fertile environment the greater their efforts to find food and so the greater our chances of catching them. But experience proves the opposite. Like salmon, the longer sea trout lie in fresh water, whether river or lake, the less interest they show in a food item or, for that matter, an angler's lure; and, needless to say, the harder they are to catch.

I refer specifically to sea trout with a sea life of one year plus, not to the young fish – the herling, whitling, finnock, smelt, sprod, scurf, truff, or what-have-you – a certain number of which undoubtedly continue to feed in fresh water as avidly as the food supply permits and which are usually very easy to catch.

By this I do not suggest that the mature fish eats nothing at all. Many adult sea trout swallow food items from time to time when these are available. (So do salmon; more than once I have watched salmon respond to a hatch of fly.) But there is a great difference between the taking of occasional food items and 'feeding'. If 'feeding' is defined as the regular taking of food for the purpose of maintaining life, then, like the returning salmon, most sea trout can, and should, be regarded as non-feeders.

It is true that, if a rise of fly occurs in river or lake, some of the fish may interest themselves; but the appearance of food is by no means a guarantee of sea trout activity. As my old friend the late T. C. Kingsmill Moore put it in his splendid book *A Man May Fish* (new edition 1979, Colin Smythe Ltd):

> 'White trout have their time of "taking", and if a rise of fly coincides with this time they will not overlook the natural, but a rise of natural will not necessarily bring them on the "take". The "take" seems to be the result of a sudden burst of activity quite unrelated to food.'

Nevertheless, despite the observations of a few enlightened writers, most people have clung to the notion that sea trout behave like their non-migratory cousins and should be approached in the same way. So, it is not surprising that, like the salmon fly, the sea trout fly got off to a rather poor start.

Most traditional salmon flies resemble overgrown trout flies because they are a hangover from the days when anglers believed that salmon fed regularly on flies, like trout did, and so tied things like big trout flies with which to catch them. And something very similar happened with the sea trout fly. Convinced that sea trout continued to feed on their return from the sea, people fished for them with the flies and methods they used for brown trout. Hence the traditional sea trout fly as we know it today, with an insect's wings and legs and tails. But of course to catch sea trout we don't need to fish flies like this at all. In fact, we shall do much better if we don't. Like modern salmon flies, some of the most successful sea trout flies haven't got these appendages; indeed, they don't look anything like natural flies.

Nothing, of course, is categorical. When sea trout are seen to be reacting to, say, a hatch of sedge, we may fish an imitation either wet or dry. At times we may simulate a nymph, or dap with an artificial 'Daddy'. The sea trout, being the diverse creature that it is, by no means conforms to a common behaviour pattern all over Great Britain and Ireland and not all sea trout waters present the same picture. In some food-rich rivers and lake systems, sea trout certainly take more interest in food than fish in spate rivers. Nevertheless, I suggest that the reason for this interest in a food item, or for that matter an angler's lure, is similar to that well-known mountaineer's interest in his mountain: *because it is there!* If it is not there the fish seldom make any effort to search for it. Like salmon they are equipped to endure a long fast while waiting to spawn and although their behaviour may vary according to their environment, few can, by the terms of our definition, be called feeding fish.

This is the similarity between the behaviour of sea trout and salmon and the difference between sea trout and brown trout. The difference between sea trout and salmon is that whereas the salmon tends to take a lure mainly by day, the sea trout – with certain exceptions, notably those of the western lakes – does so mainly by night.

Thus the concept of a non-feeding fish that takes from habit rather than hunger and is active at night is a good basis from which to think about how to catch sea trout, certainly in rivers. And the value of this philosophy, the great point to remember, is this: whether we are on a river or on a lake, since we are fishing for non-feeding fish the absence of a hatch of fly or, indeed, any surface movement, need have no effect whatever on our chances of catching sea trout.

In most of our rivers, much of the best fly fishing takes place during the hours of darkness. For many anglers, myself among them, this is the most exciting of all forms of fishing. It is also very rewarding, for I have discovered that provided fish are present and the river is not in flood (in which case daylight fishing will be in operation) there are few nights of the season when sea trout cannot be caught.

Night flies

All the traditional flies illustrated in this chapter will catch sea trout by night as well as by day but my own preference is for the lures which follow. They are mostly based on what I have observed of the sea trout's feeding behaviour in salt water and designed to stimulate a fish's feeding reflex. Many years ago, believing that returning sea trout tended to 'take' not from hunger but from habit, I experimented with lures, several of which were designed vaguely to represent creatures the fish may have been eating in the sea; lures on which I had actually caught sea trout in salt water. They were much larger than most of the traditional types of sea trout fly, but to me this seemed entirely logical.

If sea trout had recently been eating herring fry or sparling or sand-eels, as I knew was often the case, and if on their return to the river they took a lure from force of habit, then it followed that they should be stimulated by the sight of something resembling a little fish – or rather, since the sea trout had to be *lured*, something that resembled the *impression* of a little fish.

Whether my reasoning was correct does not really matter now. What did matter at the time, and what I found very exciting was that my big lures worked very well in fresh water. Indeed, they were more successful, *much* more successful, than anything I had ever used before. The rivers I fished were mainly spate streams that held only a tiny amount of food – sufficient merely to support the salmon and sea trout parr together with a tiny population of diminutive brown trout. So there was very little in the shape of insect life to stimulate the interest of a migratory fish. The big lures, fished between dusk and daybreak, struck oil at once especially with the fresh-run fish early in the season. As the weeks passed I found that a smaller fly also began to play its part.

To generalise, on all the rivers I fish today my big lures are good the season through; but, as the summer lengthens, smaller flies can be used with increasing advantage.

It is important to remember that the success of any particular fly pattern and method of fishing tends to vary from place to place. For instance the dry fly which can provide such an exciting day's fishing on some waters is comparatively useless on others. There are few sea trout waters that do not have their own well-favoured fly patterns and if the locals catch fish on them so should the visitor. Obviously these are the first to try. But many local anglers are inclined to be rather conservative and it is a mistake to think that theirs are the only flies worth using.

As I have written elsewhere, always give preference to your own fancies. What you have caught sea trout on before you will have confidence in and if you are to fish a fly with sufficient care and concentration during the long watches of the night confidence is all-

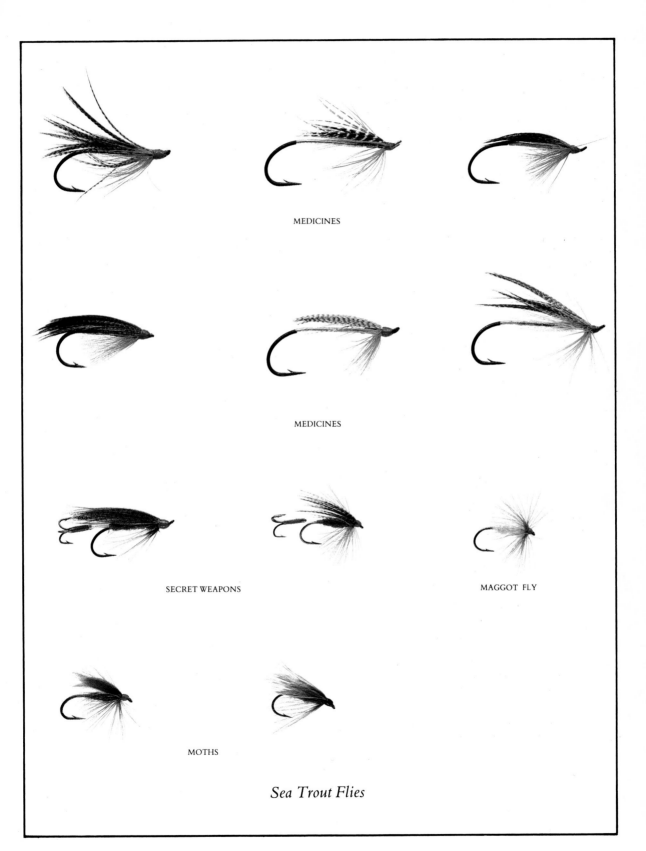

MEDICINES

MEDICINES

SECRET WEAPONS

MAGGOT FLY

MOTHS

Sea Trout Flies

important. Nevertheless, in case you care to try them, I am giving a description of some of the lures I use, since that is what I have been asked to do.

The reasoning behind these lures together with detailed notes on their construction are given in my book *Sea Trout Fishing* (revised second edition, Witherby Ltd). Sufficient here to say that both for me and many of my friends they have proved their worth during hundreds of fishing nights.

MEDICINE
Body: Silver-painted hook-shank.
Hackle: Dyed-blue cock's hackle, long and fluffed out.
Wing: Brown mallard or wigeon, sparse.
Hook: Low-water salmon, sizes 2 to 6.

This large, slim-line variant of the silver-blue can be fished all through the season on either floating or sunk line, and at all times of the night. Generally speaking, however, it fishes best in fairly streamy water from dusk until midnight. The materials used in its construction are not all-important. In some of the more peaty waters of the west, a darker fly, with black hackle, will be found more effective. It is the lure's 'flickering' impressionistic appearance that makes it attractive.

I use the largest size of Medicine on the night following a spate, or by day when the water is dark. The next night I come down a size, but seldom go below 4, even in very low water. A size 6 serves well enough at night for fly-maggot fishing; although for this technique it is better to use a Maggot Fly or, better still, a Secret Weapon.

SUNK LURE
Body: A silver-painted tandem mount, 2½ to 3 inches long, consisting of two short-shanked single hooks or two short-shanked doubles, sizes 4 or 6.
Dressing: Two blue hackle feathers, one on either side, with some strands of peacock herl on top. *Note:* It is important that the tail of the dressing does not extend past the point of the tail hook.

Fished slowly on a sunk line, this long, slim, tenuous creation will attract sea trout of all sizes late on after midnight when, so often, the fish have 'gone done'. It is especially good for hooking big fish. I have taken a number of sea trout of over ten pounds on this lure, chiefly in the small hours.

Anyone who has not experienced the power of a really big sea trout fresh from the sea may well be astonished, not to say alarmed, the first time such a fish is hooked. If it sets off at speed, as it usually does, there is nothing that can be done to stop it. Any attempt to check that first rush will result in a smash, a statement I am not going to qualify. I have known this disaster happen to too many people.

Which is why, for fishing Sunk Lure on a high-density line late at night (when a big fish is most likely to be hooked) plenty of backing is needed, and a strong leader. For myself, I never fish a big Sunk Lure on a leader of under fourteen or fifteen pounds breaking strain. This may sound heavy for sea trout, but I have been very glad of it when a double-figure fish has taken the lure in a strong current on a long sunk line and gone screaming off in the darkness.

A leader of this strength will also be found useful if a salmon is hooked – as it may be on the Sunk Lure. Indeed, this is the only lure that, in my experience, is likely to catch salmon on dark nights. Why it should do so, I don't know. But it does.

SMALL DOUBLE
Body: Silver, or black seal's fur ribbed with silver.
Hackle: Black, or brown.
Wing: Brown mallard, or grouse, or teal; straggly.
Hook: Size 12 short-shanked double.

This straggly little fly is intended as an alternative to the Sunk Lure, when sea trout are being finicky and simply tweaking. Fished late at night on a sunk line it can be surprisingly effective. The actual dressing doesn't seem to matter much; it is the size of the thing that counts, and the way it is fished. It seems to be at its best fairly late on in the season, although I have taken very fresh fish with it. *Note*: This size of double iron, with a touch of red in the dressing, is just right for a salmon late on a summer evening, or early in the morning, when the river is very low.

MOONFLY OR MOTH
Body: Chocolate chenille or brown dubbing.
Hackle: Natural hen; long and straggly.
Wing: Grouse.
Hook: Short-shanked single, sizes 6 to 8.

The Moonfly – so-called because on its first outing it caught me a ten and a quarter pound fresh-run sea trout in bright moonlight – is intended to represent something like a drowned moth. I have found it to be effective late in the season, say from mid-August, on a warm night when a bright moonlit sky suddenly clouds over.

47

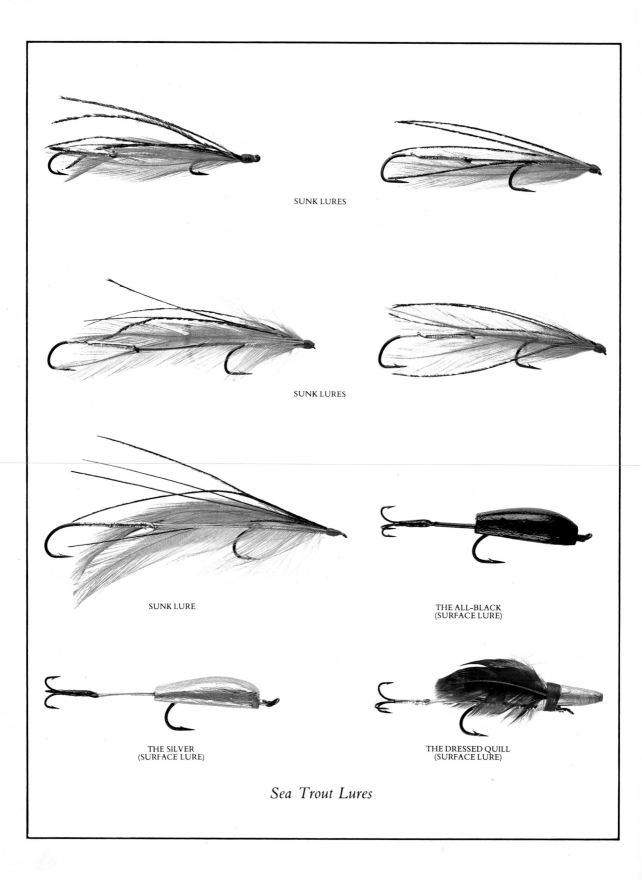

SUNK LURES

SUNK LURES

SUNK LURE

THE ALL-BLACK
(SURFACE LURE)

THE SILVER
(SURFACE LURE)

THE DRESSED QUILL
(SURFACE LURE)

Sea Trout Lures

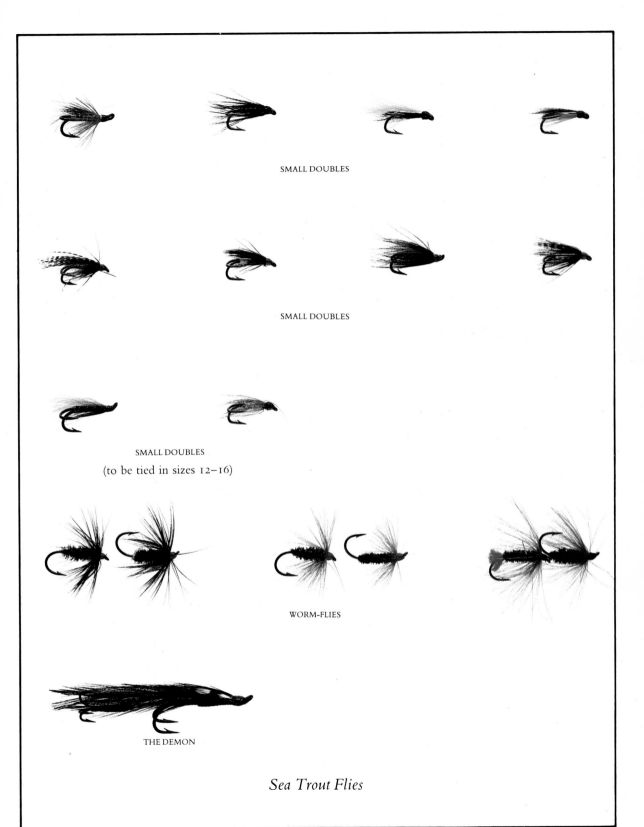

SMALL DOUBLES

SMALL DOUBLES

SMALL DOUBLES

(to be tied in sizes 12–16)

WORM-FLIES

THE DEMON

Sea Trout Flies

WORM FLY

Body: Two hooks, sizes 8 or 10, tied in tandem, each dressed with bronze-green peacock herl; length: 1¼ to 1½ inches.
Hackles: Deep red cock or hen hackles, fairly long in the fibre.
Tags: Bright red wool.

Of all the traditional or standard flies, the Worm Fly seems to me to be the best. It is a very worthwhile alternative to the Medicine in low, rather sluggish water on an August night.

MAGGOT FLY

Body: White thread, or silk, ridged.
Hackle: Brown hen.
Hook: Short-shanked, sizes 8 to 10.

There are times, particularly in low water, when the combination of fly and maggot can be very successful. The customary method is to use a small single-hooked fly with two or three maggots impaled on the hook. When sea trout are really on the 'take' this arrangement is quite satisfactory, since (together with the maggots) the hook is sucked inside a fish's mouth. But sea trout do not always take in such an obliging manner. Sometimes, usually when rain is imminent, a fish will give the maggots a tweak and let them go again, rather in the way that a salmon nips a prawn. All the angler feels is a series of infuriating little tugs. The Secret Weapon puts an end to most of this.

SECRET WEAPON

Body: Silver-painted tandem mount consisting of a very fine-wire single hook with a size 14 or 16 treble set astern. *Note:* Distance from bend of hook to tail-end of treble = ⅓ inch.
Hackle: Brown hen, well fluffed out.
Wing: Brown mallard fibres, sparse.

This lure is specifically designed for fishing two or three maggots – which are impaled on the single hook. Now, when a sea trout tweaks, it finds itself lip-hooked on the tiny treble. The Secret Weapon is fished in low water, on sink-tip or quick-sinking line, late at night when the fish are being particularly dour. *Note*: Owing to the tendency of small trebles to straighten under pressure, great care must be taken when playing a big fish.

At this point the objection may be raised that the addition of maggots to a fly does not constitute 'fly fishing'. And in a sense of course

50

this is perfectly true. But then, as I have already suggested, sea trout fishing cannot be compared to brown trout fishing, or subject to the canons embraced by that particular sport. Like salmon fishing, most sea trout fishing is *lure* fishing and does not, I think, need to be hedged by convention. So far as a sporting ethic is concerned, I submit that fishing the Secret Weapon is a highly skilled technique requiring great delicacy of touch. Anyone thinking it a too-easy method of catching sea trout should try fishing it forthwith, preferably on a dark, gusty night. They are likely to be disillusioned.

Armed with these lures we should be able to catch sea trout on most nights, provided fish are present and the river is not in flood. There is, however, a notable omission from the list without which no night fisherman should ever go to the river: the Floating or Surface Lure.

SURFACE LURE
Body: About 1½ inches long, of cork, or quill plugged with cork.

I prefer the former because, being heavier, it is easier to cast into wind.

Using doubled twenty-four pound monofil, a two-inch-long tandem mount is prepared with a size 4 single hook in front and a size 6 or 8 treble on the tail. The body of the lure is whipped to the single hook, leaving the treble trailing an inch or so behind.

Colour and dressing are unimportant. If desired, it can all be given a coat of silver paint. I usually do this simply because it looks nice. The addition of two 'wings' – any small, dark feathers will do – has no extra attraction for fish, but makes the lure more stable when it is 'swimming'.

The principle behind it is quite different from all customary methods of fly fishing. When casting across a stream in daylight, we are careful to avoid the V-shaped wake caused by a dragging fly. When fishing at night with a Surface Lure, it is precisely this drag we wish to create. It can be very attractive to sea trout.

Obviously, in order to produce a wake, the lure must be kept on the move. If, when fished across a current, the line is allowed to go slack, the lure will start to drift downsteam and drag will disappear. It is the wake of the lure and not the lure itself that seems to attract fish.

What the thing *must* do is *float*. Provided it does so, almost anything will catch sea trout. Any large, well-oiled, fuzzy dapping fly will perform as a Surface Lure. I have caught a lot of fish on a dragging Loch Ordie.

Sea trout will take the Surface Lure at any hour of the night, but the most likely period is after midnight has struck. All holding water is worth trying so long as the surface is calm enough for the lure to leave a wake. Strangely, the success of this lure varies from season to season. Some years it catches me a lot of fish, in others very few. I had thought this to be coincidence, until I learned that several of my friends have had the same experience.

The Surface Lure has a double function. It not only hooks fish, it indicates where fish are lying. Many sea trout will simply splash at the lure without taking it. Knowing their position we can, if we wish, go to work on them with something else.

But such tactics are seldom used until late at night. When starting to fish in the half-light of dusk, we kick off by choosing an appropriate size of fly – say, a size 4 Medicine.

The hour or so of dusk often inspires a burst of sea trout activity during which the fish tend to rise to a fly fished near the surface. This means that, for part of the night at least, we can fish profitably with a floating line – an altogether delightful method. Indeed, sometimes we can continue to do so with success all night. Far more often, however, we can't.

On most nights, especially when the temperature takes a dive after dark and a chill ground-mist blankets the river, fish no longer show much inclination to rise. Seemingly intent only on their breathing, they lie near the bottom and remain indifferent to a fly that passes high overhead.

You may wonder why they should take a fly at all late on a cold night. The answer is that (with the exception of the Surface Lure, which may tempt an occasional fish to come to the top) they won't – unless the fly is fished deep and slow.

This means that in order to give ourselves the best chance of catching sea trout, we should be prepared to fish a fly fairly fast and close to the surface at dusk; and, later, when the sea trout have gone down, to fish it slowly, close to the bottom. As a result, since both floating-line and sunk-line tactics are likely to be used during the same night, our minimum tackle requirements will be a suitable fly rod and two lines: floating line and sinking line. A better arrangement – to save messing about in the dark changing reels – is to use two rods, one fitted with a floater, the other with a sinker.

A typical fishing night may be split up into three periods: from dusk until approximately midnight; from midnight until, say, one o'clock in the morning, and from then until daylight. The first period, to use a sporting metaphor, I call the 'first half', the second period 'half time', and the third period the 'second half'. There is also a brief period at daybreak that will sometimes produce a fish or two – I call it 'extra time'.

It will be found that roughly sixty per cent of the sea trout caught during a season's fishing will be taken in the first half; about ten per cent during half time, and about thirty per cent during the second half and extra time. But it is worth noting that the second half produces a bigger average size of fish.

Of course, these figures must not be taken too literally. They are intended simply as an indication of what to expect. On some nights, fish may be caught only during the first hour. On others, not until perhaps two or three o'clock in the morning. Very occasionally the fish may stay on the 'take' all through the night and a large bag made. But such nights are rare.

With the exception of those clear, cold evenings of swirling ground-mist, when the temperature drops sharply with the setting sun and we may start by fishing deep with sinking line, it is likely that floating line tactics will be in operation during the first half. That sea trout usually take best of all during this period there can be no argument. But after some exciting action lasting for anything from half an hour to, say, an hour and a half, they are likely to stop taking and 'go down'. At least, that is the pattern on most nights.

This sudden cessation of sea trout activity is the start of what I call 'half time', and there is never any doubt when it happens. The fish themselves 'blow the whistle' and the river seems suddenly lifeless. It is at this point that so many people lose heart. Thinking the fish are 'off' for the night, they take their tackle to pieces and go home.

They may be right. But on most evenings they will be wrong.

It is now, at the start of 'half time', that the question of whether returning sea trout remain active feeders proves to be so important. When the fish go down, anglers whose approach is based on satisfying the hunger of feeding sea trout regard further fishing as being pointless. Certain in their own minds that the fish are 'off the feed', and that sport must therefore be over for the night, they pack up, thus denying themselves many chances of catching fish, especially the bigger fish!

Without doubt the sea trout are down, and it is likely they will stay down. But that doesn't mean they cannot be caught. Indeed, unless there is a dramatic change of weather and the river starts to rise, there will almost certainly be many opportunities of catching sea trout all the way through until daybreak and after provided we change our tactics in sympathy with the sea trout's change of behaviour. That is, we change from fishing our fly fast near the surface to fishing it slowly near the bottom.

I have suggested that, over a season, the period after midnight will produce the bigger fish. This, I think, is due partly to an aspect of the sea trout's night time feeding behaviour and partly to our tactics during the second half, which will consist mainly of Sunk Lure and Surface Lure fishing. These lures sometimes tempt big fish that smaller lures have failed to move.

That the period when we need to fish deep with a Sunk Lure should also be propitious for Surface Lure may seem contradictory. But darkness is all-important for surface 'wake' fishing, and on many nights early in the season it is never really dark until after midnight.

As I mentioned earlier, there is not only the chance of catching big sea trout in the early hours, there is the chance of a salmon. I have taken quite a few salmon with a two-and-a-half to three inch Sunk Lure in low, clear water late at night, and so have several of my friends. So far, we have done so on nine different rivers. I am not referring to those conditions of midsummer twilight experienced on northern Scottish rivers, but really dark nights from mid-July onwards. The usual taking times have been between one o'clock and about three-thirty. If there was a moon, thick cloud covered it. One well-remembered fourteen pounder took in moonlight diffused by high cloud. The air temperature seems to have little effect. On several occasions I have caught salmon when the river was shrouded in dense ground-mist.

Most major salmon rivers have big runs of sea trout, and for the angler who is not exhausted after a day's salmon fishing there is every chance of sport with sea trout at night. Clad in breast waders he will encounter few problems when fishing the long, broad pool tails of a big river, and all the methods described here should serve him well.

In addition to these, there is an exciting method of fly-fishing at dusk known as 'casting round-the-clock'. In effect, it is a stillwater boat-fishing technique applied to the river.

Make up a leader with one dropper. Tie a Medicine or some other slender fish-like fly on the tail, and a hackled fly – a Kingsmill Moore Claret Bumble will do admirably – on the dropper. Soak the dropper-fly in Permaflote.

Wade carefully into the tail of a pool to a position from which fish can be covered with a fairly short line, and stand perfectly still. Start by casting upstream at an angle of, say, ten o'clock to the opposite bank. As

54

soon as the leader touches down, draw in the flies by raising the rod and stripping line with the non-casting hand. Work them so that the tail-fly fishes just below the surface with the bob-fly dragging along on top, leaving a wake. Don't let the flies stop or slow down but recover them in the same smooth movement and cast again. This time from ten to, say, eleven, and so on 'round-the-clock'.

If a fish rises but refuses, don't cast over it again too soon. Make several casts well away from it in other directions first.

Very slowly, make your way upstream, casting as you go.

The best fishing time is the late dusk of a warm summer night, when the river is low and the sea trout are widespread over the 'flats' or near the tail of a big pool.

An eleven- or twelve-foot single-handed carbon rod is ideal for this form of fishing which, in my opinion, provides the only sensible opportunity of using a dropper at night. Droppers are a curse in the darkness, especially in a gusty wind. But with the short line used for round-the-clock fishing, a bob-fly can be very effective.

It is advisable to land a hooked fish on the spot. With a little thought and practice this can be done very easily, provided landing-net, priest and fish-bag are slung ready to hand.

When the fish is played out and safely in the net, carry out the following drill:

1   Hold the net handle between your legs and pull some line off the reel. This is to avoid jerking the fly – which is either still in the fish's mouth or, if it came away when the line was slackened, is entangled in the net.

2   Get the rod out of the way by stuffing the butt down inside your breast-waders.

3   Reach for the priest and knock the fish on the head while it is still in the net.

4   Unhook the fish, take it by the gills and slip it into the waiting fish-bag.

5   Re-sling the net.

As well as avoiding the disturbance of wading to the bank and back again each time a fish is landed, dealing with it on the spot will save time – which is very valuable during those all-too-brief periods when sea trout are really on the take. One word of advice, however. Never try to do anything too quickly at night. Every movement, whether we are wading or changing a fly, should be deliberate and unhurried. As I know from bitter experience, being too hasty in the darkness can lead to some terrible tangles!

Stillwater fishing

So much has been written about fishing in stillwater that to describe it in detail would be repetitious. I have, however, one brief comment that may be helpful. The customary method of moving to the upwind end of a fishing area and then drifting downwind is not really very effective. A fish that rises 'short' will sometimes take the fly if given another chance; but all too often, before this fish can be covered a second or third time, the drifting boat is swept over it.

Far better, in my experience, is to have the boat rowed slowly and carefully on a course *across* the wind, moving gradually downwind in a series of 'legs'. These legs will be long or short according to the relation of wind direction to the fishing area (see diagram).

Much hangs on the skill of the oarsman. When a 'hot-spot' is reached, the boat is checked and held in position. This allows the 'lie' to be covered several times without fish being frightened by the sight of the boat.

A variation of casting angle, fly depth and speed of recovery adds spice to boat fishing. Rowing across the wind enables considerable changes to be rung in fly presentation, besides being especially helpful when the bob-fly is feathered along a wave.

Stillwater flies for sea trout

A great number of traditional fly patterns are available for stillwater fishing and opinion will differ as to which are best for any particular water. R. C. Bridgett, who delved into the matter in detail, examining the records in fishing hotels and questioning tackle dealers, came up with the following list of most popular sea trout flies in the 1920s:

Butcher	Silver Doctor
Peter Ross	Grouse and Claret
Teal and Silver	Pheasant and Yellow
Dunkeld	Blae and Blue
Mallard and Claret	Blae and Black

His list for the Hebridean lochs was as follows:

Teal and Silver	Mallard Claret and Yellow
Mallard and Claret	Woodcock Teal and Yellow
Hen Pheasant and Yellow	Black Zulu
Butcher	Blue Zulu
Silver March Brown	Black and Silver

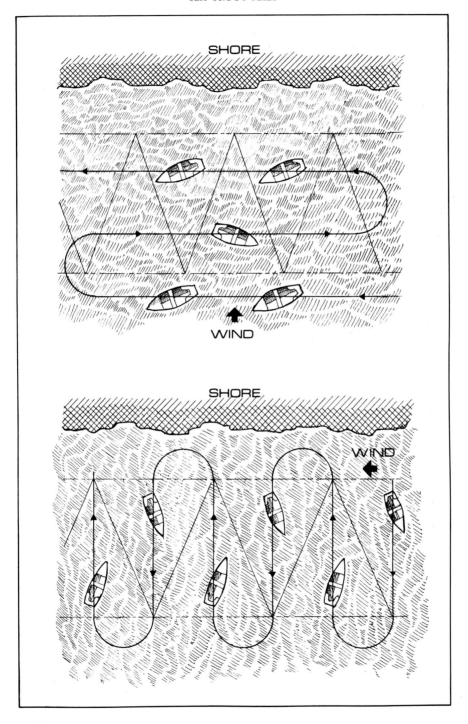

For Connemara, he suggested:

Blue Zulu	Alexandra
Blae and Black	Bloody Butcher
Hen Pheasant and Yellow	Brown Turkey
Mallard and Claret	Grouse and Claret
Mallard Claret and Yellow	Connemara Black
Black and Silver	Thunder and Lightning (Irish)

That famous angler, Hamish Stuart, author of *The Book of the Sea-Trout* (c. 1917), who did not favour a large range of patterns, always used the same three flies when loch fishing. These were:

Tail fly: Mallard and Claret
Middle: Woodcock and Green
Bob-fly: Zulu

'This may seem carrying the principles of the "little range" too far,' he wrote. 'Yet if sea trout are at all in the mood these flies will "kill".'

Among other patterns he recommended were: Teal and Blue; Grouse and Purple: Cinnamon and Gold; Butcher.

The following is a fairly comprehensive range. They are all proven killers and at some time or other I have caught sea trout on every one of them. A combination of two or three flies from this list should serve for any water in the British Isles.

Tail flies

Mallard and Claret	Black and Silver
Grouse and Claret	Dunkeld
Grouse and Purple	Fiery Brown
Woodcock and Green	Brown Turkey
Butcher	Cinnamon and Gold
Bloody Butcher	Silver March Brown
Peter Ross	Invicta
Teal and Red	Pheasant and Yellow
Teal Blue and Silver	Woodcock Teal and Yellow
Alexandra	Thunder and Lightning

Additional Tail flies

The Kingsmill (see page 60)	(Both Medicine and Sunk Lure can
Medicine (sizes 4 to 6)	be useful in wild weather, fished on
Sunk Lure (two-inch)	sink-tip or quick-sinking line.)

Bob-flies

Black Zulu Blae and Black
Blue Zulu Blae and Blue
Black Pennell Connemara Black
Claret Pennell Kingsmill Moor Bumbles

Here are the dressings:

MALLARD AND CLARET
Tail: Golden pheasant tippet.
Body: Dark claret seal's fur ribbed with gold.
Hackle: Natural black and red.
Wing: Dark mallard.

GROUSE AND CLARET
Tail: Golden pheasant tippet.
Body: Bright claret seal's fur ribbed with gold.
Hackle: Dyed bright claret.
Wing: Grouse.

GROUSE AND PURPLE
Tail: Golden pheasant tippet.
Body: Purple seal's fur ribbed with oval silver.
Hackle: Black cock.
Wing: Grouse

WOODCOCK AND GREEN
Tail: Golden pheasant tippet.
Body: Green seal's fur ribbed with gold.
Hackle: Red hen.
Wing: Woodcock.

BUTCHER
Tail: Red ibis.
Body: Flat silver ribbed with oval silver.
Hackle: Black hen.
Wing: Blue-black mallard.

BLOODY BUTCHER
Tail: Red ibis.
Body: Flat silver ribbed with oval silver.
Hackle: Bright red.
Wing: Blue-black mallard.

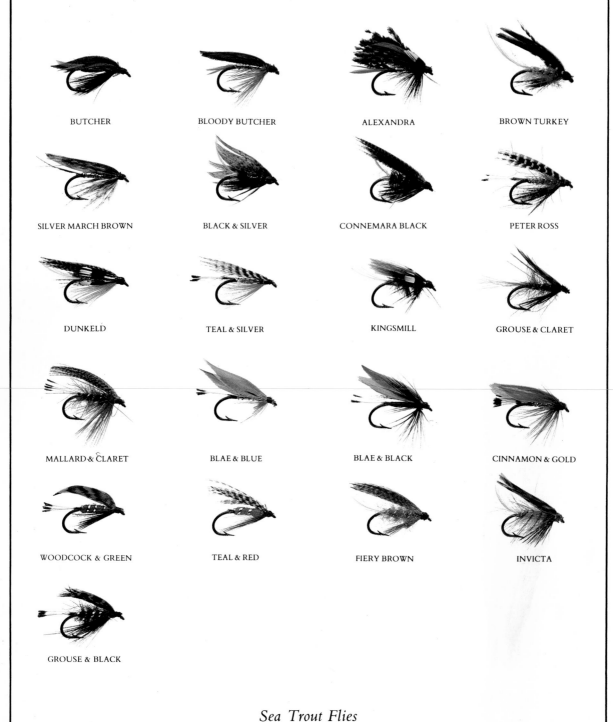

BUTCHER

BLOODY BUTCHER

ALEXANDRA

BROWN TURKEY

SILVER MARCH BROWN

BLACK & SILVER

CONNEMARA BLACK

PETER ROSS

DUNKELD

TEAL & SILVER

KINGSMILL

GROUSE & CLARET

MALLARD & CLARET

BLAE & BLUE

BLAE & BLACK

CINNAMON & GOLD

WOODCOCK & GREEN

TEAL & RED

FIERY BROWN

INVICTA

GROUSE & BLACK

Sea Trout Flies

PETER ROSS
Tail: Golden pheasant tippet.
Body: Half flat silver, half red seal's fur ribbed with oval silver.
Hackle: Black hen.
Wing: Dark teal.

TEAL AND RED
Tail: Golden pheasant tippet.
Body: Red wool ribbed with oval silver.
Hackle: Dark brown cock.
Wing: Teal.

TEAL BLUE AND SILVER
Tail: Golden pheasant crest.
Body: Flat silver ribbed with oval silver.
Hackle: Dyed blue.
Wing: Teal.

ALEXANDRA
Tail: Red ibis.
Body: Flat silver.
Hackle: Black.
Wing: Peacock herl with red ibis and white tipped mallard.

BLACK AND SILVER
Tail: Golden pheasant crest; Indian crow; tipped oval silver; light orange silk; ostrich butt.
Body: Half flat silver; half black floss ribbed with oval silver.
Hackle: Black with jay at shoulder.
Wing: Fancy mixed.

DUNKELD
Tail: Golden pheasant crest.
Body: Flat gold.
Hackle: Dyed orange.
Wing: Dark mallard, jungle cock cheeks.

FIERY BROWN
Tail: Golden pheasant crest; orange tag.
Body: Brown seal's fur ribbed with oval gold.
Hackle: Brown cock.
Wing: Brown mallard.

BROWN TURKEY
Tail: Golden pheasant crest.
Body: Yellow and red claret seal's fur.
Hackle: Black and red cock.
Wing: Brown turkey with strip of teal; fibres of golden pheasant tippet under wing.

CINNAMON AND GOLD
Tail: Golden pheasant tippet.
Body: Flat gold ribbed with oval gold.
Hackle: Cinnamon.
Wing: Cinnamon.

SILVER MARCH BROWN
Tail: Light mallard.
Body: Light hare's ear ribbed with flat silver.
Hackle: Partridge.
Wing: Mottled hen pheasant.

INVICTA
Tail: Golden pheasant crest.
Body: Yellow seal's fur ribbed with oval gold.
Hackle: Brown hen wound head to tail; blue jay at throat.
Wing: Hen pheasant.

PHEASANT AND YELLOW
Tail: Red macaw.
Body: Yellow seal's fur ribbed with oval gold.
Hackle: Blue jay.
Wing: Hen pheasant.

WOODCOCK TEAL AND YELLOW
Tail: Golden pheasant tippet.
Body: Yellow seal's fur ribbed with oval gold.
Hackle: Red hen.
Wing: Woodcock and strip of teal.

CONNEMARA BLACK
Tail: Golden pheasant crest; tipped oval silver, and orange floss; peacock butt.
Body: Black seal's fur.
Hackle: Jay or Guinea fowl.
Wing: Brown mallard.

THUNDER AND LIGHTNING
Tail: Golden pheasant crest; tipped oval silver and orange floss.
Butt: Black ostrich herl.
Body: Black floss ribbed with oval gold; dyed orange hackle down body.
Hackle: Jay.
Wing: Brown mallard with jungle cock cheeks; golden pheasant crest over all.

BLACK ZULU
Tail: Red wool tuft.
Body: Black wool ribbed with flat silver.
Hackle: Black hen.

BLUE ZULU
Tail: Red wool tuft.
Body: Black wool ribbed with flat silver.
Hackle: Dyed light blue.

BLACK PENNELL
Tail: Golden pheasant tippet.
Body: Black floss ribbed with fine oval silver.
Hackle: Black cock.

CLARET PENNELL
Tail: Golden pheasant tippet.
Body: Claret seal's fur ribbed with oval gold.
Hackle: Black cock.

BLAE AND BLACK
Tail: Red ibis.
Body: Black seal's fur ribbed with flat silver.
Hackle: Natural black.
Wing: Duck.

BLAE AND BLUE
Tail: Red ibis
Body: Flat silver ribbed with oval silver.
Hackle: Dyed blue.
Wing: Duck

Last of our historical dressings is a fly that has just come to my notice: The Best, which a Scottish Album of 1868 claims: 'Will kill almost anywhere'.

I have not yet had a chance to test this claim, but the fly looks a good 'un. Here is the dressing:

THE BEST
Tail: A short tuft of orange-yellow floss silk.
Body: A dark ruddy-brown or brown-red (something like the colour of red hair) pig's wool; fine silver twist.
Hackle: Coch-y-bondhu.
Wing: Two strips of bright teal.

The writer also lists another fly, The Best No. 2, which is given a body of bright orange with a black hackle.

And now for the Kingsmill. This excellent tail-fly was invented by the late T. C. Kingsmill Moore. Many years ago he sent me one to try out and I caught a lot of fish on it, both in still water and in the river.

Here is the dressing:
Tail: Golden pheasant topping.
Tag: Blue floss (RHS enamel blue 48/1★), tied rather broad and prominent.
Body: Black ostrich herl, ribbed oval silver.
Hackle: Best quality black cock; if your cock hackles are thin or chalky, use black hen.
Wing: Rook secondary, closely rolled so as to keep solid, and tied long, low, and rather narrow.
Sides: Jungle cock, small and not too white in the enamel.
Topping: A good golden pheasant topping, taken hard up against the top of the wing, and long enough to intersect the topping at the tail.

Next, some brilliantly successful stillwater bob flies: the Kingsmill Moore Bumbles.

Of the seven patterns of Kingsmill Moore Bumbles whose dressings I give, the Claret Bumble is my favourite. Of this fly, Kingsmill Moore writes:

'This is an outstanding pattern for white trout, and I must have taken over 800 on it.'
Tail: Four strands of golden pheasant tippet.
Body: Medium claret seal's fur (RHS. Indian lake 826/3), ribbed oval gold.
Body hackles: Cock dyed medium claret, and natural black cock.
Shoulder hackle: Blue jay.

★Royal Horticultural Society's two volume colour chart.

64

GOLDEN OLIVE BUMBLE
Tail: Golden pheasant topping.
Body: Golden olive seal's fur, ribbed oval gold tinsel.
Body hackles: Cock dyed golden olive, and medium red natural cock.
Shoulder hackle: Blue jay.

THE BRUISER
Tail: A bunch of flax-blue wool.
Body: Rich gentian blue wool (RHS gentian blue 42 or Prince's blue 745/1), ribbed silver.
Body hackles: Cock dyed gentian blue, and natural black cock; these are taken the whole way to the head.
Shoulder hackle: None.

'Especially good on a dark day with low clouds and showers,' comments Kingsmill Moore. 'The hackles are wound rather closer than in the other patterns and the fly is less transparent, so that its bulk may show against a dark sky.'

FIERY BROWN BUMBLE
Tail: Indian crow.
Tag: (Optional) golden brown floss.
Body: Fiery brown seal's fur, ribbed oval gold.
Body hackles: Fiery brown and blood red cock (RHS blood red).
Shoulder hackle: Dark grouse.

'A fly chiefly for coloured water. I am not quite satisfied with this dressing, but have not been able to improve it.'

GREY GHOST
Tail: Golden pheasant topping.
Tag: Black ostrich herl.
Body: Light grey seal's fur (or silver monkey), ribbed oval silver.
Body hackles: Dyed Irish grey cock (much the colour of a pale blue dun) and a natural black cock hackle.
Shoulder hackle: Teal, or grey partridge.

'There are days when there is a milky look on the water usually caused by an east wind haze, and other days of diffused light when under-water visibility seems much accentuated. Fishing is rarely good in these conditions, and the best thing to be done is to change to a finer cast, use a very small black fly at tail and a larger light coloured fly at dropper. This fly is also worth trying on very bright sunny days.'

SILVER BLUE BUMBLE
Tail: Golden pheasant topping.
Body: Closely wound, fine, oval silver tinsel.
Body hackles: Bright medium blue dyed cock (RHS Butterfly blue 645) and natural badger cock; they should be wound rather open.
Shoulder hackle: Teal.

MAGENTA AND GOLD BUMBLE
Tail: Orange toucan.
Body: Closely wound, fine, oval gold tinsel.
Body hackle: Magenta.
Shoulder hackle: The pink-cinnamon hackle from the wing of a landrail.

'These two flies are bumble patterns of Teal Blue and Silver and of Freeman's Fancy respectively. They have a limited use for fresh run white trout, in low water and bright sun . . . The silver is better in July and the gold in August.'

Sea trout fly fishing offers splendid opportunities for the fly tyer to experiment with various colour combinations and degrees of dressing. Indeed, for many of us, one of the joys of the sport is to experiment; to try out different creations. Very occasionally we may strike a brief period of inexplicable success when, in one particular time and place, some whimsical offering unexpectedly rings the bell.

I remember an astonishing week, years ago on one of the western lakes, when a friend and I hit lucky with a bright orange lure of doubtful pedigree tied originally for reservoir fishing. The sea trout took this streak of orange with great gusto. They would take nothing else. It was uncanny. For several days, no other type of lure we proffered hooked a single fish.

After that I tried the orange lure everywhere I went, confident that one day it would repeat its magic. It never did.

The reason for such perversity? I simply don't know. Sea trout are the most complex and mysterious of fish, forever capable of doing the unexpected. Often enough, just when I thought I had them all worked out, they have turned my theories upside down.

After a lifetime's experience of these strange and wonderful creatures, I have learned one great truth – that I understand very little about them.

Reservoir flies
and fishing

GEOFFREY BUCKNALL

Geoffrey Bucknall is married with two sons and lives at Bromley in Kent. He owes his fly fishing life to growing up in the Weald of Kent, during the last war, when a friendly farmer with a stretch of trout stream indoctrinated him with the cult of the dry fly. Later, he widened his experience, and has written some nine books on fly fishing, as well as contributing to books and magazines at home and abroad.

Some years ago, due to changes in his health and work in a medical laboratory, he started his own fly tying firm. From this has grown three successful firms in fishing tackle manufacture, wholesale, and retail trading.

Fly fishing apart, he has wide and diverse interests, which include boats, large motor-cycles, linguistics, bull terriers and apple-growing.

It is necessary to state at the outset that I am concerned here with large waters. The problems of fly fishing in wide tracts of water are entirely different to those of smaller put-and-take fisheries. The reservoir allows space and time in which stocked fish can develop a wild response to natural food whereas the confined and heavily stocked small fisheries contain trout, however large, which have been unable to shake off the artificial conditioning influences of the stew pond. In stating these differences I am not necessarily implying criticism of the latter, for both fisheries fill certain needs. Any trout fishing is better than none. However, to believe that trout from confined put-and-take waters pose the same challenge as the large lakes would involve an element of self-deception which I find unacceptable.

This preference for the large waters imposes the problems with which I must deal. The first problem is that of tackle and casting. And let us accept that we are forced to recognise that, for the most part, distance casting is essential. To prove this beyond question, let me cite two typical factors. The first is the marginal shallow, characteristic, say, of Grafham or Chew lakes, where you can still see the lake floor for many yards in

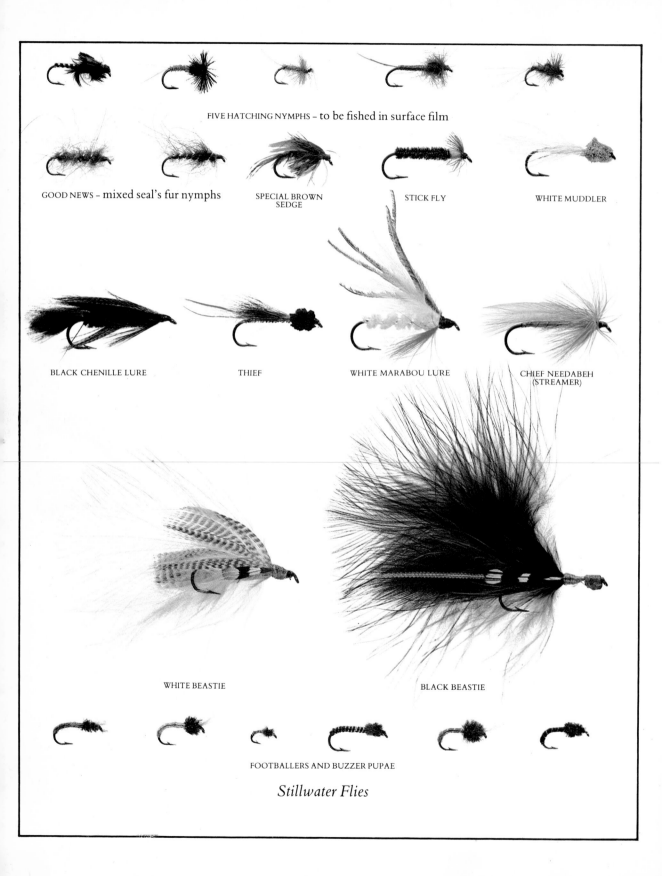

FIVE HATCHING NYMPHS – to be fished in surface film

GOOD NEWS – mixed seal's fur nymphs

SPECIAL BROWN SEDGE

STICK FLY

WHITE MUDDLER

BLACK CHENILLE LURE

THIEF

WHITE MARABOU LURE

CHIEF NEEDABEH (STREAMER)

WHITE BEASTIE

BLACK BEASTIE

FOOTBALLERS AND BUZZER PUPAE

Stillwater Flies

BLACK LURE

BADGER LURE

TODD TANDEM

SWEENEY TODDLER

SQUIRREL & ORANGE

WORM FLY LURE

'Dick Walker' Reservoir and Lake Flies

front of you, with rising trout yet further out still. The other extreme is the very deep reservoir, an example of which is Datchet, where it is vital to throw a very long sinking line just to reach the feeding depth of the fish.

Distance casting depends on two things: tackle and technique.

The correct distance fly casting technique is the double haul, scaled down from tournament usage to a more practical and less critical routine than that required for ultimate performance on the casting platform. We should aim at a fatigue-free double haul routine which can be maintained for long periods to give a working distance of at least forty yards.

Space constrains me to describe the double haul routine briefly, but it is simply the normal overhead fly cast with two hauls of line with the free hand, plus a feedback between them. Each haul roughly coincides with the rod sweep, back cast and forward cast with the line feedback on the pause between these two movements. The first haul overcomes the line's inertia and straightens it in the air. The second haul gives the line speed in the air prior to the considerable shoot at the climax of the forward cast.

In practical fishing these two hauls can be fairly gentle, sweetly flowing almost into each other, and with a little practice and the development of timing, it is not necessary to keep turning the head or body to watch the line to the rear. This falls into place, with muscle memory, or, to use golf terminology, it becomes 'grooved in'.

Stillwater fly fishing became specialised after the war, largely due to the efforts of anglers like the late Cyril Inwood and T. C. Ivens. Until then, there had been little in the way of the development of imitative or practical fly patterns. Northern lochs, for example, had been fished successfully with scaled-up versions of river and sea trout flies. Experience alone sorted out favourable patterns, the Mallard and Claret, Butcher, Blae and Black, for instance. Of course, these flies must have had some rough relationship to stillwater fly life, but in fishing in a mixed team while drifting before the wind in a boat, it would be sufficient to allow the fish to sort out this problem. Thus, for instance, if the trout consistently took the Blae and Black, only the very rare thoughtful angler would relate this to the black buzzer. This could not go on, the inquiring mind being what it is and, after the Second World War fly design went in two different directions.

Inwood and Ivens, for example, were impressed with the physical behaviour of their fly patterns, and although the new series of nymph patterns bore an approximate relationship to natural nymphs (Black and

Peacock Spider, Green Nymph, Brown Nymph, etc,), they were also intended to fish at chosen retrieve speeds and depths, and streamlined to serve the needs of long-range casting. Other anglers, though, such as John Goddard and C. F. Walker, were proceeding along the lines of close imitation. As it happened, my own small contribution to stillwater flies took a middle path, with the invention of the Footballer.

In the early sixties I had made my first visit to Blagdon, and being caught by prolific buzzer hatches, fishless in the famous 'Blagdon Boil', I had recognised the shortcomings in the so-called buzzer patterns of the day, which consisted of fly bodies made of tinsel around smooth silk bodies. The pronounced segmentation and hook-like shape of the natural buzzer pupae were absent, as were effects to simulate the thorax and wing-cases. The short answer was to collect specimens of the natural, have photographic enlargements made to analyse the prominent features, and then to make a copy which could be fished in a lifelike way.

The segmentation was achieved by winding a strand of black horsehair together with a strand of clear, side by side over white silk. The hook-shaped abdomen was easily copied by starting the segmented body half-way round the hook bend. The thorax was a pinch of dubbed mole's fur, and the head was a few turns of bronze peacock herl. I left out the sophistication of breathing tubes, gills, and tail filaments, in order to make a fly which could be cast accurately to a cruising trout, cutting cleanly through the surface film to intercept it. I must confess that this was done to serve a personal fishing preference for attacking fish seen to be rising or surface-cruising.

The wide size variations of natural buzzer pupae on various waters were easy enough to achieve by hook choice, but although the standard Footballer copied that popular striped variety, it did not cope with other prominent colours, such as red, orange, black, etc. It was not long, though, before I had used clear horsehair or nylon over fluorescent silks with teased-out wool thoraces to match. It must be remembered that these patterns emerged slightly before the more sophisticated copies fly tyers delight in today, but the fully imitative effect was left out of my own thinking – and still is – because I have always thought it intelligent to relate the fly to its behaviour in the water as well as its appearance in our own eyes on dry land! The great weakness of close imitation, as well as in the arguments of those who discuss fly line, fly rod or fly leader colour, is that we do not know exactly how and what a trout sees. There is enough evidence to suggest that they see colour and shape differently from the way we do. You only have to imagine the broken glitter of a

Pupae

BLACK

GREEN

OLIVE

OLIVE

ORANGE

Corixae

LARGE BROWN
(leaded)

LARGE BROWN
(unleaded)

SMALL GREEN
(leaded)

SMALL GREEN
(unleaded)

OLIVE NYMPH
(leaded)

OLIVE NYMPH
(unleaded)

AMBER NYMPH

DRY CINNAMON
SEDGE

Polystickles

BROWN (8)

BROWN (6)

GREEN (8)

GREEN (6)

ORANGE (8)

ORANGE (6)

Wet Trout and Reservoir Flies

WICKHAM'S FANCY

CINNAMON & GOLD

ALEXANDER

BADGER

TEAL & GREEN

BLACK SPIDER

BLACK GNAT

BLACK MIDGE

HARDY'S FAVOURITE

INVICTA

BLAE & BLACK

PHEASANT TAIL

RED SPINNER

STONE FLY

RED HACKLE

COCH-Y-BONDHU

HARE'S LUG

COW DUNG

DUNKELD

TEAL BLUE & SILVER

WOODCOCK & HARE'S EAR

SNIPE & YELLOW

TUP'S INDISPENSABLE

BRACKEN CLOCK

OLIVE DUN

Wet Trout and Reservoir Flies

rippled lake surface in sunlight to know that this must be true.

The lesson of this is two-fold. It means that the older schools of fly fishermen were right in two ways. Firstly, the lessons of experience as applied to traditional fly patterns are valuable. The Mallard and Claret will go on killing trout, and it does not really matter why. Secondly, the way in which a fly behaves is more important than its actual shape, colour, and size, in relation to the natural fly.

The post-war period also witnessed the extension of lure fishing, which, curiously, was mainly an importation from America. True, the first popular lure was probably the Jersey Herd, in its dual rôle as a true fry imitation and also as a provocative lure in its own right. The original Jersey Herd took its name from the coppery milk-bottle top from which its body was made, though later versions reverted to plain gold tinsel. The true dressing involved a torpedo-shaped underbody over which the copper tinsel was laid. A bunch of bronze peacock herl formed back, tail, and head, with a hot-orange hackle.

Funnily enough, plastic-bodied fry imitations along similar lines had a brief vogue, then died on us, and it was not until Don Gapen's Muddler Minnow came along that the lure fishing fashion really exploded. The secret of the standard brown muddler lies in both its drab colours and its large air-trapping head of cropped deer-hair. The dull overall colour, with just the slightest flash of gold, is important for, with a few exceptions, small fish are also sombre in their camouflage – obviously they have to be – and true minnow imitations must be likewise. The head-up effect of the Muddler made it perfect for fishing with fast sinking lines over weed beds, along dam walls and other sunken obstacles.

Another paradox was that lure fishing needed a lure with a head-down effect, and it was the application of the very lively marabou turkey feather which made this possible with the invention of the Beastie, one of my other rare contributions to fly tying history. This idea came to me from a friend, Dr Tony Richards, who, when fishing with me at Hanningfield, occasionally clipped a large swan shot to the head of a normal marabou lure. I was struck by the way in which this used to add considerable sinuosity to the wing of the lure, and sophistication followed.

The resulting family of Beastie lures had two layers of lead wire wound over about a quarter of an inch of the long shanked hook, at the head. The main wing was made of two almost-whole marabou plumes tied back-to-back, with cheeks of silver pheasant flank feather on either side. The wing extended at least as twice as long as the hook shank, and the effect of the weighted head was to make this tail vibrate, while the lure would rise and fall according to the retrieve pattern. It soon became obvious from the sheer violence with which Hanningfield and Grafham trout hit the Beastie lures that we had another powerful killer to act as a perfect foil to the Muddler family.

Above all, both Muddlers and Beasties demonstrate the importance of the way in which flies and lures behave in the water, a factor which is overlooked in the general hypnosis caused by mere variations in colour which pour out of the inventive minds of angling writers, almost week by week. From a practical point of view, if we reject the concept of exact imitation, it is then possible to rationalise a simple system of flies for reservoir fishing. In the two cases I have discussed, that of the buzzer imitation and the new structures of lure, we have covered a wide spectrum of fly needs, but we need to add a practical nymph system.

The system which I use is based on the predominant colour of the natural, and hence the artificial aquatic fauna. In making an artificial nymph we have to think carefully of the aspect of the material we use for the structure. There can be no doubt that, in spite of many modern man-made fibres such as polypropylene or mohlon, seal's fur is by far the most attractive, for not only does it refuse to absorb water, but it retains its ability to reflect light underwater in myriads of tiny filaments of shining colour.

The best use of seal's fur involves the blending of various colours. Of course a predominant colour is needed, say olive, or black, amber, orange or brown, according to time of the year and the prevailing activity of certain types of natural food-life. In my experience, the other two contrasting colours are not so important providing that they contrast vividly with the main colour, which should be twice the quantities of the other two. It is wise to mix uncut strands of seal's fur and to avoid the American idea of chopping them up in food-blenders, because the longer strands can be picked out either at the thorax, in the case of the orange or amber nymphs, to copy sedge pupae, or all along the underside of the pale olive version to copy the Fresh Water Shrimp.

Now let me put this into practical context. These nymphs are dressed on long-shanked hooks, say size 10 or 12. For deep fishing, the bottom half of the hook is lapped in lead wire. Three colours of seal's fur are mixed together, the strongest colour predominating in a proportion of two-to-one. For example, if an amber nymph was needed, then you may add, say, some strands of scarlet and green to the amber, then mix

ORANGE HAIR WING MISSIONARY

MISSIONARY

APPETIZER

DARK WING MISSIONARY

WHITE MARABOU MUDDLER

BLACK MATUKA

BLACK & ORANGE MARABOU

ACE OF SPADES

JACK FROST

BLACK BEAR

SINFOIL FRY

JERSEY HERD

Wet Trout and Reservoir Flies

WHISKEY

BROWN LURE

WHITE LURE

SILVER BADGER

BABY DOLL

GOLD FLY MINNOW

CARIBOU (WHITE)

CARIBOU (ORANGE)

STRIPEY

YELLOW PERIL

Reservoir Flies

the three colours well together. The mixture is dubbed onto the hook shank, thickening up at the thorax, and the longer strands picked out as previously described. A fine oval gold ribbing is added, and this completes a very simple family of nymphs first introduced to me by a friend, Bill Robins. Their great virtue lies in their simplicity, versatility to be fished at any speed and depth, and their colour variability.

The lure and nymph variations are very wide, and I have selected just a narrow sector of the going market; though in the case of nymphs, the vast proportion of still water food, namely buzzer and sedge, is very well catered for in my choice, and is all that I ever need to carry with me. There are two other groups of flies to be considered, the traditional patterns, and dry flies. Either of these would merit a book in its own right.

Certain traditional patterns of fly have killed fish on stillwater for decades. Such a pattern is the Mallard and Claret, and it is hard to relate it to natural fauna on many lakes, except, perhaps that many of us darken the claret seal's fur body with mole's fur, which brings it very close to the black and dark buzzer nymphs. Other patterns relate definitely to certain insects. It is easy to spot a connection between lake olives and Greenwells, black buzzer and the Blae and Black, sedge pupae and Invictas, for example. It must also be true that certain flashy, tinsel-bodied flies provoke trout in the same way as do brightly coloured lures. The Dunkeld, Butcher, Peter Ross, and Wickham obviously fall into this category.

Perhaps the most underrated aspect of stillwater fly fishing is the dry fly. This is strange because the ability of a well-collared hackle fly, such as the Black Pennell, fished as a top dropper or bob fly, can often bring up trout when the fly is worked in the surface film when drift fishing on any large lake or loch. This reaction to a surface commotion could be looked at either as the trout thinking an insect were on the point of hatching, breaking free from its nymphal shuck, or else believing it to be a terrestial creature, such as a moth or daddy-longlegs, blown into the water from the land, and struggling to break free from the clinging surface film. Even so, the explanation may still be too complex. It may simply be an instintive reflex to movement and broken light; who knows?

The use of the bob-fly is not confined to the surface boil at this fly itself, for in being attracted to the surface disturbance of the bob fly, the fish may well come to a lower fly in the team, a process known as 'bringing the fish up'. In this sense, too, it is intelligent to fish a larger, flashy fly as the anchor man, above which is a smaller nymph it appears to chase, thus setting up the competitive urge of the trout to intervene in a minor predatory struggle, however artificially contrived.

What of the dry fly proper? As far as artificials are concerned, they are mostly concerned with terrestial insects like moths, daddies, ants, hawthorn flies and the like, or truly acquatic insects such as sedges, which are intercepted by trout either as these flies hatch, or as they return to lay their eggs on the water. Here I must speak in general terms, for there are many local variations, some lakes even having hatches of mayfly, an example of which being where the infant Tone joins the mighty Clatworthy reservoir.

The drift of fly life from the land is obviously due to the offshore wind, and the angler would position himself accordingly. Trout will swoop in close to take the daddy, and the huge swirls and presence of the fly in the air are plain enough signs. The fishing of a moth at dusk, though, is a matter of prospecting and pure chance. I try to make a deliberate wake with such a pattern as a large Hoolet. This copies the brown moths by having a plump peacock herl body topped off with two natural red game cock hackles and a rolled wing of brown owl. It is exciting to watch the fly being pursued on the surface by the furrow of a surface trout, to watch it finish in the angry boil and feel the surge as the big fish hits it.

Dry sedge flies are similar to river patterns, my favourite being the normal Cinnamon Sedge, the body of which is cinnamon turkey herl with body and throat hackles of red cock, a fine gold wire rib and a strip of brown feather for the rolled wing. The age-old argument as to whether or not to move the floating fly is easily solved by trial and error. Sometimes the fish want to chase the fly, on other occasions they do not; it is that simple.

Most of us fit dry fly fishing into a selection of reservoir tactics, but anyone wishing to specialise in this type of fishing might scale down his outfit to a light, fast-actioned rod to throw a finer floating line. I have had some success in dry fly work, and sub-surface nymph fishing, by dying black the last twelve inches of fairly long leaders. As in all fishing where you cast accurately to intercept visible fish, providing you use a long leader and go to work carefully, the colour of the fly line is completely unimportant.

Dapping is another form of dry fly fishing, and if I were lucky enough to fish one of those great Irish loughs where it scores heavily, I would adapt a telescopic roach pole of some fifteen feet for that work. It is, of course, the art of tripping a large, bushy fly across the wavetops (or even naturals). Just occasionally, when English reservoir trout are really on to the daddy-longlegs, I adapt my normal rod, tying in a very long leader. About a yard above the fly I hitch into the nylon a butterfly of tissue paper, which catches the wind and helps to carry the fly before the boat. It is a makeshift substitute for the floss silk or nylon blow lines made specially for the job.

I make special dapping bi-visible flies by palmering one colour of hackle over a contrasting colour, one going up the hook shank, the other down to lock it. Thus the hackle points spread in many directions for extra support and the killing colour combinations – red and black, olive and orange, white and red – can all be made into simple dapping flies, with a few extra turns at the throat for support.

These are the basic flies and methods for reservoir fly fishing, the lure, the nymph in its broad sense of the word, the teams of traditional wet flies, dry fly, and dapping. You have to fish, and my final word is, as always, that the fish is the only critic who counts in the end.

The dry fly

JOHN GODDARD

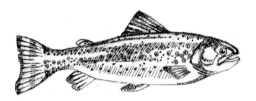

One of our most popular and successful trout fishers, John Goddard is also an author of many books on trout fishing, as well as being a regular contributor to many of our piscatorial publications. Involved in angling all his adult life, he is a past vice chairman of the Angling Trade Association, and past chairman of the Angling Foundation. A skilled macro photographer, his work on flies both natural and artificial is in constant demand.

The history of dry fly fishing has been well documented over the last century or so. Despite this there is still considerable controversy as to who first developed the technique of fishing the dry fly as we know it today. From the dawn of fly fishing history, fishermen have endeavoured to present their flies on the surface where the trout were seen to be feeding, and it was doubtless the sheer weight of the early, relatively crude, hooks which foiled possible attempts to float the artificial. It was during the first half of the nineteenth century that fishing with a floating fly first came into vogue, and it may be significant that this coincided with the development of lighter, more sophisticated hooks.

I have now been fishing the dry fly for well over twenty-five years and still enjoy the delights and challenge of this particular branch of our sport as much as I did when I first started. However, I would be less than honest if I did not admit that at one period I became totally absorbed in fishing the upstream nymph and was convinced that this required much more expertise than fishing the dry fly, and there is little doubt that this is so, as the dry fly need only to be presented in two dimensions, while the nymph must be presented in three. With both methods, length and breadth must be taken into account, but with the nymph, judgement in depth also has to be assessed – which is far more difficult. To become a top-class nymph fisherman requires many years of constant practice, and at least initially, it is essential to have a good tutor to explain the basic techniques. In this respect I was very fortunate to have as a friend the late

Oliver Kite, whose skill at this form of fishing was positively uncanny, and I would like to think that at least some of his expertise eventually rubbed off on me. It is only in the last few seasons that I have begun to realise that, while fishing the dry fly may require less expertise, a really difficult trout feeding on surface flies offers much more of a challenge than a similar trout feeding underwater on purely aquatic forms of life.

Now how do we overcome this challenge, but first of all, exactly what is it? With both forms of fishing, observation, approach and presentation are of paramount importance, but when fishing the dry fly as opposed to fishing the nymph one has, in addition, to take into account the choice of pattern. As there are literally hundreds of dry fly patterns to choose from, one is faced with an additional challenge that is both interesting yet often frustrating and which will only be overcome, hopefully, by presenting an acceptable pattern in an acceptable size.

Let us now take a brief look at the development of dry flies since their inception in the first half of the last century. Most of the very early patterns were superseded by more efficient and effective creations developed towards the end of the last century. This was undoubtedly the golden era of the dry fly, as it was during this period that the cult of the dry fly was rapidly gaining ground, culminating with the appearance of Frederik M. Halford, whom today most fly fishers look upon as the father of the dry fly. Certainly he had a very forceful character and through his many books and articles to the angling press he dominated the fly fishing scene in his late years and was largely responsible for instigating the 'dry fly only' purist approach that to some extent is still with us to this day. The many patterns he developed during his lifetime were the most beautiful creations of fur and feather, but sad to relate, few, if any, are well-known today. On the other hand, many eminent fly dressers who were operating during this period, particularly during the 1880s, perfected patterns that are still household names today. During the early part of this century, professional fly dressers such as Powell, Wooley, Austin, and Hanna introduced many exciting new patterns, but most of these were dressed by conventional methods. By the 1920s traditional dry flies were beginning to change. William Lunn, a famous river keeper on the river Test, introduced an exquisite range of spinner patterns, J. W. Dunne introduced his sunshine dry flies based on his painstaking studies of translucence in natural flies, and these were followed by such innovations as parachute hackles. Since then, steady progress has been made, particularly in the last decade or so, due to the introduction of a multitude of new synthetic materials, many of which have virtually revolutionised the art of fly dressing. In this period encompassing nearly one hundred and fifty years, many thousands of patterns have been perfected, and, although many of these have now been forgotten in the mists of time, it still leaves several hundred dressings for the angler to choose from, including, of course, many from countries outside the UK, so where does one start? Certainly it is a daunting task, even for the relatively experienced dry fly man. Most of us seem to solve this problem by collecting flies like confetti and finish up with boxes and boxes of flies, most of which will never be annointed with floatant and cast upon the water. In the hope that it will prove of some value, I have been persuaded to provide a basic selection of artificials that will at least ensure one has a reasonable choice of patterns to offer trout throughout the season on any dry fly river or stream in this country. I hope it will be appreciated that the list is my own personal choice, so please forgive me if I have left out any of your personal favourites. While the list includes many modern, and even some American dressings, many old and famous names also appear, as these are just as effective now as they were on the day when they were first invented. The list is in alphabetical order, and brief details of the history and usage of each pattern is given.

THE ADAMS

Perfected and popularised by Leonard Halladay of Mayfield, Michigan, this is one of the older traditional general dry fly patterns that is still very popular both in the USA and Canada. Dressed in the smaller sizes 14 and 16 I have found it to be a fine floater and consequently a wonderfully effective pattern in fast or broken water where it is often difficult to see or follow most English patterns which are, by comparison, very sparsely dressed.

THE BLACK GNAT

While there are many different dressings to imitate these tiny black flies of the same name, I now favour the new dressing recently perfected by Brian Clarke and myself as detailed in our new book *The Trout and the Fly*. Dressed on a tiny hook it is a very lifelike pattern and has proved to be very effective.

GOLD RIBBED HARE'S EAR

A traditional pattern that has been popular for many years. It may be dressed with or without wings according to personal taste. Strictly speaking it is not really a dry fly as it fishes in the surface film and was designed to represent the nymphs of the various species of olives

87

hatching through the surface. As such it is a very effective and useful artificial to carry as when trout are so engaged they will often ignore the adults drifting along on the surface and likewise any dry flies meant to represent them.

GREY FOX VARIANT

The brainchild of the well-known and respected American fly dresser Art Flick, this is indeed a super pattern to have in one's fly box when the caddis flies are hatching. The long hackles recommended for this pattern ensure that it floats very high above the surface. Fished with a little movement it skates across the surface in a most enticing manner, copying to perfection the struggles of a freshly hatched sedge fly in its efforts to become airborne. I assure you most trout find it irresistible, particularly at dusk.

GREY DUSTER

This is an excellent general pattern, and it seems to be equally effective whether it be fished on the river Test or a brawling mountain stream in Wales or Scotland. A very useful fly to carry in your box, especially when any small natural flies are hatching. The original dressing did not have any tails, but Donald Overfield, the well-known fly dresser, suggests tails should be included and I am inclined to agree.

THE HAYSTACK

This is a new pattern developed by that gifted fly dresser Stewart Canham to represent the mayfly, our largest ephemerid. It looks like nothing on earth, but does it catch trout! As a general mayfly pattern it has no equal, and in addition it has two great merits. It will literally float all day, even in the roughest of water, and it is also an extremely durable dressing. Stewart's original tying had a grey polypropylene body with cream calves' tail, hair wings and tail and a grey hackle. After some experimentation, I found that grey hair for the wings and tail and a buff coloured polypropylene body with black hackle was even more effective and that is the dressing I now use.

THE HUMPY

This is another excellent and well-known American pattern that was developed from an original idea by Jack Horner of San Francisco. The basic material used in this pattern is deer's hair, a bunch of which is used for the tail, body and wings, a clever but difficult pattern to dress. I find it is a most useful pattern dressed in the smaller sizes as it floats so well, particularly in fast or broken water. Strange to relate I find it most

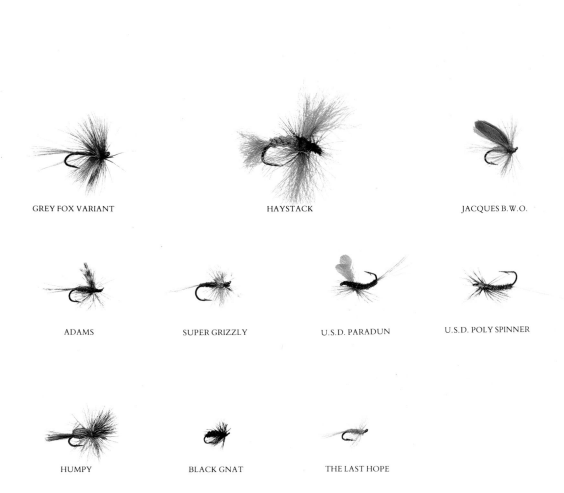

GREY FOX VARIANT   HAYSTACK   JACQUES B.W.O.

ADAMS   SUPER GRIZZLY   U.S.D. PARADUN   U.S.D. POLY SPINNER

HUMPY   BLACK GNAT   THE LAST HOPE

Dry Flies

effective during the latter half of the season, when sedges are hatching, although I am sure its author never originally intended it as a representation of the adult caddis flies.

THE IRON BLUE DUN

This is one of the older traditional artificials meant to represent the natural fly of the same name. It should always be dressed on small hooks, size 16 to 18, and it is an extremely effective pattern particularly early or late in the season during wet or cold days which, for some odd reason, seems to favour the hatches of the tiny natural flies. Trout seem to be inordinately fond of them, and a nicely dressed and presented artificial will often create great execution, even on days when hatches of the natural are sparse.

JOHN STOREY

A very popular general pattern in the north country where it originated during the middle of the last century. The original dressing was intended for wet fly fishing, but as the dry fly became increasingly popular, it was modified accordingly. Like many of the old traditional patterns that have stood the test of time, this fly was invented and modified by a famous river keeper.

JACQUES BLUE WINGED OLIVE

Most fly fishers appreciate that trout feeding on Blue Winged Olive duns are notoriously difficult to deceive, and no fly dresser has yet managed to evolve an artificial that is consistently successful. However, this pattern, developed many years ago by David Jacques, the noted author and amateur angling entomologist, comes very close, and I would certainly not be without it in my fly box.

LITTLE RED SEDGE

A pattern that was developed at the beginning of this century by G. E. M. Skues, one of the greatest and most observant fly fishers of all time, must surely warrant a place in one's fly box. When sedge flies are active towards dusk in the latter half of the season, this is a wonderful artificial and has tempted many a specimen trout from the calmer, slower stretches of water where the trout are able to see it on the surface from a considerable distance.

THE LAST HOPE

One of my older patterns that has become increasingly popular over the years, it has deceived many large and difficult trout for me, and I now tend to look upon it as my sheet anchor when trout are feeding on any small flies. It was originally developed to imitate the small pale watery dun of early summer, but I consequently found, dressed with a dark body, it was equally effective later in the year when small dark olives were hatching. The paler bodied dressing has also accounted for countless numbers of trout feeding on the dreaded caenis on both rivers and lakes.

THE P.B. MAYFLY

This is a more recent innovation of my own, tied specifically to represent the mayfly dun. A Veniard plastic mayfly body is utilised and with this fitted over the shank and then sealed so it is watertight it provides a very buoyant and lifelike pattern. It has certainly sealed the fate of many large, selectively feeding fish, and over the past two seasons I have tended to reserve its use for the more difficult trout, using Canham's Haystack pattern for the general run of trout as it is far more durable and equally effective on non-selective feeders.

PHEASANT TAIL SPINNER

This well known general spinner pattern has, over the years, provided me with many a good trout. Invented in or about 1901 by a Mr Payne Collier, there are many different dressings, but the one I favour is that suggested by the great G. E. M. Skues and is as follows. Several strands of honey dun for the tails, followed by three strands of ruddy pheasant tail fibres for the body, which is ribbed with gold wire. The hackle of rusty dun cock should be bright and sharp.

SUPER GRIZZLY

A new artificial recently developed by myself, it was designed as a general pattern for Mr Average Trout. In this guise it has proved a resounding success, taking trout on many different waters throughout the country under varying conditions. It is important to dress this pattern with good quality bright and sharp hackles.

THE U.S.D. PARADUN

A very successful pattern developed by Brian Clarke and myself to deceive the more difficult trout, it sits high above the surface on a reversed parachute hackle. It may be dressed in various body colours and sizes to represent the many species of upwinged duns. A difficult fly to dress, it should be reserved for those few very special trout.

THE U.S.D. POLY SPINNER

A worthy partner to the above dun, this new pattern is dressed on a keel hook to ensure correct presentation. The polythene wings are dimpled and viewed from below the surface in the mirror reflect sparkles and flashes of light, as do the wings of the natural spinners. The trout seem to find this new pattern irresistible, and we have enjoyed great success with them. As in the dun, it may be dressed with different body colours and in various sizes to represent any particular species of spinner.

TERRY'S TERROR

Another general dry fly pattern, dressed on a very small hook it will take trout feeding upon natural Iron Blues, and on a large size hook it will even do duty as a sedge. Invented by Dr Cecil Terry of Bath, it has in latter years been popularised by the well-known fly dresser Peter Deane who considers it the best all round pattern he has come across since he started dressing flies in 1948.

Dry Flies

WINGED OLIVE

GREY DUSTER

GREY HEN & RUSTY

BLAE & BLACK

PURPLE & ORANGE

BLUE QUILL SPIDER

WICKHAM'S FANCY

GREENWELL'S GLORY

MARCH BROWN

PARTRIDGE & YELLOW

BADGER & RED

IRON BLUE & PALE EVENING

Nymphs

OLIVE

PHEASANT TAIL

BLACK BUZZER

BLAE & BLACK

GROUSE & CLARET

MARCH BROWN

Dry Flies and Nymphs

Wet flies for
river trout

WILSON STEPHENS

Wilson Stephens was editor of The Field *for twenty-six years and of* The Salmon and Trout Magazine *for five years, partly concurrently. He is the author of the best-selling* Guinness Guide to Field Sports, *has edited the fly fishing books of Frank Sawyer, was consultant and a major contributor to the international production* Hunting *(Marshall Cavendish Publications), wrote the sport and wildlife sections of* Encyclopaedia Britannica *and writes regularly in many publications under several pseudonyms. But he much prefers fishing to writing about it. He has fished in ten countries, from North America to India, but is happiest on quick upland British trout streams, where he can hear curlews calling.*

The essence of old simplicities sets the tone of most pleasurable human experiences. For many of us, 'wet fly down' is where fly fishing began, and historically it is the tap-root of the sport. Around it, and latterly dwarfing it, the specialised arts of the dry fly and of still waters have increasingly captured anglers' attentions. And yet, as it was 'in the beginning' remains a compelling formula. To repeat the phrase is to feel the visions grow of all that these three words evoke, and lost worlds coming back.

Wet fly down means hills – the Western moors, the Welsh mountains and the March, the Pennine dales, Scotland, and lonely streams in Ireland's faraway west. Wet fly down means open skies and brisk winds, lively water, clear sounds and bright colours. From all around comes the bleating of sheep. Curlews bubble, buzzards mew, dippers fly past and perhaps a ring ouzel whistles. Purple heather at the water's edge, or the land golden with broom and whin. A man can be alone there, yet feel the companionship of nature. And if perchance he raises a thirst there will be an inn to slake it where fishermen are as much part of the scene as the buzzards and curlews.

Wet fly down is no way of breaking records. This is the scene where men of old would fish in well-cut knickerbockers, the water not being wide enough for wading, with wicker creels to hold their catch of breakfast-sizers, among which a half-pounder would add both tone and substance. Sometimes, of course, one can do better. I have had pleasant surprises. But, in the main, wet fly down is a small operation in a wide setting where the reward is proportionate not to what a man gets out of it, but to what he puts in – his soul, for instance.

A wet fly river man, not being likely to catch fish worth talking about to others, fishes for his own contentment in a self-contained way. This element of concentration leads me to regard wet flies in a manner very different from my attitude to floating flies. In the latter case the fly and the fish are both visible. I can see what happens, and what does not. The relationship of cause and effect, monitored by observation, is as clear as an engineering sequence. Not so with the wet fly. Once under water, it is in a world of its own, dispatched on a specific errand. Dry flies are tools of the sport, wet flies are personal emissaries. The difference elevates the wet fly from the status of ammunition to that of partner.

In other ways also the art of the wet fly fisherman is one of constructive imagination. His reading of the water is an example of it. The interplay of currents, the humps and eddies on their surface, tell him the topography of the stream's bed. From this he deduces the likely whereabouts of fish. Every cast he makes is the miniature replica of a salmon cast in which some part of his ego leaves him and travels the arc of the underwater world in company with the flies he has sent there.

This personal element in the relationship of the fisher to his flies gives special character to their nomenclature. Whereas dry flies and nymphs tend to be named in recognition of the insects which they represent, wet fly names are often those of their inventors, or reflect some folklore of the land of their origin. Interpreting them often requires knowledge of local dialects. Misinterpreting them is apt to arouse fierce regional loyalties. Let every man beware of unintentionally belittling some gift to posterity evolved on a stream to which he may be a newcomer, thus showing insufficient respect to a heritage conferred by one who walked its banks before him.

As an example, the supreme wet fly of all time, perhaps the most honoured artificial fly of any kind embodies this principle of 'let us now praise famous men', and is justly claimed as a Geordie creation by the robust and proud fishers of North Eastern England. Moreover it expresses the mystery and magic, even the contempt for such a trifling concept as science, which is central to the joy of the wet fly Greenwell's Glory. The name says it all.

When he escaped from his pastoral cares in Durham for some spring fishing on the Tweed in 1854, Canon Greenwell had neither forewarning nor intent that he was about to add a masterpiece to the already long list of trout flies. However he saw, or thought he saw (being a truthful man, he did not overstate his claim), a particular natural fly being freely taken, and with the help of a local fly tyer, James Wright, designed the now famous pattern in imitation of it. The formula was simple: wings, inside of a blackbird's wing; body, yellow silk cobbler-waxed to give a greenish-olive hue; hackle, coch-y-bondhu. The consequences were global. What the natural fly was has never been determined, so the artificial one expresses the separateness of wet fly fishing from the concept of exact imitation.

Nowhere in the world where flies are cast for trout is Greenwell's Glory less than an article of faith. There can be few fly-boxes on this planet which do not contain at least one Greenwell. I have met it in a Norwegian Fjord, on mountain streams in Austria, in Yugoslavia, Italy and France, across the Atlantic in Newfoundland and on the American mainland, in Asia on the Himalayan glacier waters. Sometimes it works miracles. Night-fishing on a Connemara estuary where the outflowing river was porter-brown with peat, I had put up a Butcher, hoping that starshine reflected from the silver body would act as an attractor amid the encircling gloom. Shuffling footsteps and heavy breathing in due course told me I was not alone. Only time would reveal whether I was being joined by cow, ass, or fellow-being.

The latter it was. He was upwind, and had not been abstemious during the evening.

'What have ye on?' came a thick voice. I told him.

'Mercy. 'Tis over bright.' There were sounds of still heavier breathing, and of varied contortions. 'I've a Greenwell here (more breathing) if I can just have it off-hooked from me vest.' I never argue with local advice.

The feat was performed, the flies changed in discreet torchlight, and the Greenwell dispatched in conditions which, in or out of water, seemed well fitted to make its sober hues invisible. Within half an hour two sea trout were on the bank, one of which my benefactor took home, along with his treasured Greenwell, safely re-anchored in his vest, whatever that may have been.

It is fitting that good deeds should be rewarded, especially among such deserving people as anglers. Canon Greenwell, having conferred his great boon upon millions of his fellow men, was granted long life in

ROYAL COACHMAN

PARMACHENE BELLE

KING OF THE WATER

CARDINAL

MCGINTY

BEE

BEAVERKILL

QUILL GORDON

DARK CAHILL

GREY HACKLE PEACOCK

JOCK SCOTT

SILVER DOCTOR

DARK MONTREAL

PROFESSOR

RUBE WOOD

Chompers

ORANGE

OLIVE

GREEN

BROWN

RED

WHITE

Hardy's American Wet Flies

COCH-Y-BONDHU

BLUE DUN

BLUE UPRIGHT

MARCH BROWN
(female)

WOODCOCK & YELLOW

ALDER

MALLARD & CLARET

BLACK PALMER

COACHMAN
(hackle)

GREENWELL'S GLORY

SNIPE & PURPLE

PATRIDGÉ & YELLOW

PETER ROSS

Wet Flies for River Trout

which to enjoy it. He fished for another sixty-four seasons, which spanned from the Charge of the Light Brigade until the end of the First World War, and in his ninety-seventh year was still happily catching trout on his inspired invention.

Inspiration indeed it is which makes good wet flies. By comparison, dry fly design is mere police work; accumulate the evidence and act accordingly in imitation, that is the process. This would never do for wet fly fishing. In this there is no evidence to what or why the trout react, only intuition. In the application of this sixth sense as distinct from scientific data, some personal humility plus sensitivity to what might be dismissed by less discerning men as a passing thought, has motivated many others.

The names of those who have given their identity to famous flies form a roll-call of those fitted to stand on some heavenly podium beside the blessed Greenwell himself. They make a varied host – Peter Ross (now who was he?), Holmes of the dark sedge (a doctor who likewise fished by night), Rolt of the witch (a Victorian commuter-fisherman from South London), Brookes the Ludlow postman, Broughton the Penrith shoemaker whose 'Point' has been a favourite in Cumbria for a hundred and fifty years, Bradshaw the inventive Yorkshireman, Tod the most talented wet fly man ever, and very many more. And I wonder who invented the indispensable Waterhen Bloa?

It is not enough for the wet fly man to know the masters of design, and to perfect his technique in presenting their creations. There remains the art of the tyer. In no sphere of fly fishing is this more crucial. Upon the execution of the formula depend the sub-aqua dynamics of the fly when fished. In the hand, a wet fly lies unmotivated. The tension created by the pull of the stream against the control of the rod tip brings it to life. Left to itself, it would be swept past fish after fish like any piece of detritus; energised, it suggests vitality and, because of that, acquires seductive power.

For these reasons, with the single exception of 'beetle fishing', an important tactic on Welsh mountain streams, my strong preference is for winged patterns over the hackled variety. Admittedly wings, if the word is taken literally, are anachronisms under water. But they are not intended to be taken literally, by anglers or by fish. They are essential to the paravane character of a well-tied wet fly and, more than anything else, decide its performance in the presence of fish.

The slope of the wings, when aligned by the tension of the leader to the flow of the stream, has the effect of submerging the fly and causing it to twist and swerve, as if burrowing its way against the current as would small creatures of the underwater world, such as nymphs and fry. To be useful, therefore, a fly which is to be fished wet must be streamlined. The wings must be tied in with enough 'hump' to deflect the fly downwards, but no more. In no other respect must its outline bulge.

The hackle with which it is tied should be from a hen, of whatever species. Female filaments are softer, more responsive to the passing touch of water, hence more suggestive of life. In addition, none of the components of a wet fly should be in excess. Just enough, not a strand more, is ideal. If more is used the impression of vitality is reduced, as with an over-weight athlete. It often seems to me that the besetting sin of all fly tyers who are not active anglers (which means most of those commercially employed) is that their flies are over-dressed – whether for wet fly, dry fly, or salmon. Canadian fly tyers are superior to British in this respect.

My personal link with the flies I use leads me to think of them as being grouped on a regional basis, it being accepted that, wherever I go, Greenwell's Glory goes too. In the Pennines I would not be without Broughton's Point, Dark Needle and Waterhen Bloa. This latter name, bewildering to southerners, arises because the fly expresses in its small compass the basic character of 'dales' fishing. No dictionary has told me officially what 'bloa' means; I can only deduce it from its context in conversation with farmers and shepherds on those hard, high hills which stretch from the Leeds-Bradford conurbation north to Cumbria and the Cheviots. There its meaning is close to that of 'bloat' in the sense that a 'bloa' day is one which leaves one blue with cold. By association, the bloa flies are those which embody in their body tying the shades characteristic of a complexion deadened by cold. As such they seem appropriate to their region.

The fishermen of Yorkshire and Lancashire are also enthusiasts for the needle patterns. Paradoxically needle flies tend to hatch on warmish days, so seem more characteristic of the langorous south than the brisk north. Again, however, I do not believe that the tying is intended to represent fidelity to a natural insect. More likely, it seems, that these slender patterns, having originated in early Victorian times when dark-coloured Toledo steel was fashionable for the needles used in Britain, were so named because of their own prevailing steely hues.

The doctrine of streamline is less observed in the Welsh Marches, the land of beetles, bumbles and similarly tubby creatures and their artificial counterparts. Most famous of all is the Coch-y-bondhu, mean-

RED PALMER   SOLDIER PALMER   SILVER INVICTA   CONNEMARA BLACK

GREENWELL'S SPIDER   BLUE ZULU   BLACK ZULU   WATSON'S FANCY

COACHMAN
(winged)   MARCH BROWN   GOLD MARCH BROWN   SILVER MARCH BROWN

MARCH BROWN SPIDER   GROUSE & CLARET   BUTCHER   BLOODY BUTCHER

BLUE DUN   BLUE QUILL   IRON BLUE DUN
(male)   IRON BLUE DUN
(female)

BLACK PENNELL   BLACK & PEACOCK SPIDER   PETER ROSS   WOODCOCK RED & YELLOW

WOODOCK GREEN & YELLOW   TEAL & YELLOW

Wet Flies for River Trout

ing in English 'red and black', the colours of the natural beetle. It is represented by a wide range of artificial versions of which the Palmers, the Hackled Red Tag and the old-fashioned Marlow Buzz have done me good service.

West Country fly fishing is dominated by the natural species of March Brown and Blue Upright. Trout conditioned to these and their nymphal stages fall for the Dark Snipe and Purple – especially if fished high in the water late in the day and allowed to hang beside patches of scum (if hanging be possible, which it generally is not). On Dartmoor and Exmoor Teal and Yellow often attracts better than the conventional hackle March Brown, perhaps because of the evident attractive power of the barred teal feather, which occurs in more than a hundred wet fly patterns.

Ireland seems a land of red-orientated trout. Claret and Mallard is generally my opening bid there, with Gold-ribbed Hare's Ear at first reserve especially if really soft-hackled. My fishing in Ireland led me to distrust the widely followed custom of fishing wet flies in teams of three, as in lake fishing. The only advantage which this confers on me is the fun of picking the teams. Against this it provides three times the risk of a fankle, or of being hung up. On moving water I prefer the single fly, and believe it more efficient in the long term.

Except that in each case the flies are fished sub-surface, little relationship exists between wet fly fishing in rivers and stillwater fly fishing. The one notable exception is provided by Scotland. There my fly selection for river or burn fishing is precisely what I would use for drifting a loch – but half the size. People tell me that I am very eccentric in this respect; perhaps so, but the system works.

For simplicity, here is a table of 'standard' flies and the times of the year when they are most useful:

Pattern	Size	Natural	Period
Waterhen Bloa	14	large spring olive	March/April and September
Waterhen Bloa	16	small dark olive	March/May and September
Orange Partridge	14	March brown, some stone flies	March/May and September
Snipe and Purple	16 & 18	spring black (gnat) and iron blue dun	March/June and September

Pattern	Size	Natural	Period
Dark Snipe	16 & 18	spring black (gnat) and iron blue dun	March/June and September
February Red	14	small stone fly	March/April
March Browns (various)	12 & 14	March browns	March and early April
Snipe and Yellow	16	medium olive	April to June and September
Dark Snipe	16	medium olive	April to June and September
Dark Watchet	16 & 18	iron blue dun	late April/June and September
Dark Needle	16	small stone fly	April/June and September
Brown Owl	16	small sedge or stone fly	April/June
Black Gnat	16	small gnat	May to end of season
Poult Bloa	16	pale watery dun	May to end of season
Crimson Waterhen	16	small red spinner	May to end of season
Knotted Midge	16	black midges mating	May to July
Rough Bodied Poult	16	blue-winged olive dun	late May to end of season
Green Insect	16 & 18	aphid (greenfly)	June to end of season

Recognised patterns of wet fly in Britain number more than four hundred. It is impossible to name them all; impossible, too, to wear them all round my hat. I would do so, if I could. For without denigration to any other form of fly fishing, and perhaps only for the sake of the places to which it has taken me, wet fly down has given me as much private pleasure as the rest put together. In these days of bigness – big fish, big numbers, big money – there are still many of us for whom this old style remains the cream of the sport. It was good enough for the Roman soldiers, who cast the first recorded artificial flies; good enough for Izaak Walton and Charles Cotton; it is more than merely good enough for me.

Flies for lake
and stillwater

DEREK PATTINSON

Derek Pattinson was born near Gosforth in West Cumbria where his family have been well-known for several generations.

He has devoted his life to country pursuits so it is perhaps natural that he should have chosen land agency as a career, handling the affairs of such great estates as Lowther in Cumbria. He also is a considerable landowner in his own right.

Derek is not only a first-class shot and dedicated horticulturist but a lake fisherman of such distinction that he represented England for many years in their annual matches against Scotland on Loch Leven. It is a matter of considerable distress for his Scottish friend Douglas Sutherland that during all the years that he represented England, Scotland rarely managed to win.

The reaction of anyone when asked to write 'as an expert' on a subject so controversial as fishing must be to feel a natural hesitancy. Who is to say that one man's methods are better than another's? Or how often is the 'expert' confounded when a comparative novice 'wipes his eye'?

I am somewhat reconciled to my task by the fact that I have been asked to write about lake fishing for, of all forms of fishing, to me lake fishing is the supreme pleasure.

Like, I am sure, every other contributor to this book, I have practised every known form of the fisherman's art and derived the greatest enjoyment from doing so; yet my fondest memories are of days spent on lake or loch.

Possibly I have been luckier than many for a great deal of my fishing has been on the beautiful lakes of my native Cumbria, with frequent raids over the Border to the wild grandeur of Scottish lochs, from Loch Leven itself, a mecca for fishermen from all over the world, to the most remote of Highland tarns.

Beautiful surroundings are very much part of a fisherman's enjoy-ment and where better to enjoy than drifting gently on the surface of a lake? Even the presence of other boats does little to spoil the feeling of peace or the sense of freedom. The fisherman on the river bank is limited by the extent of the beat and other restricting factors which do not apply to the lake fisherman. For him the lake and the ever-changing colours of landscape, the drifting clouds above and the fitful moods of the wind on the water are a world of his own.

A more practical advantage of boat fishing is that it is so much more comfortable; a real consideration as the years creep on. Some years ago, I took an old friend of mine, the late artist J. D. Kenworthy, out on Loch Leven. He fished every day for a week and caught more fish than anyone else on the loch. He was ninety-three years of age.

Of course conditions are not always as ideal as I have portrayed them and have a habit of changing with remarkable suddenness. He is a wise man who is prepared for anything. My fishing 'wardrobe' consists of good thick sweaters, mitts and warm stockings, a sou'wester or a broad-brimmed felt hat, gum boots, and a waterproof cushion.

The type of boat, too, is of great importance. A well-built clinker boat, with a deep draught to keep it steady in rough weather, is ideal. A boat of fourteen or sixteen feet long and a good width will sit steadily in the water without constantly turning, and allows plenty of room for rods casting at either end.

The length of rod depends largely on the characteristics of the water to be fished. On Loch Leven, for example, fish often rise very close to the boat and a short rod, say about nine foot six, is a great advantage when one has to strike quickly. On the other hand, with a longer rod, it is easier to work the bob fly, which is an important element in loch fishing.

I have never been an advocate of the extremely long cast. I doubt if it raises any more fish and certainly a higher proportion are lost through the difficulty of controlling the strike. I am a great believer in working the fly slowly and using a sunk line, drawing the flies back along the line of the cast by raising the tip of the rod or pulling in the slack by hand, depending largely on conditions. With the trout rising freely one should fish more quickly and nearer the surface.

Covering all the water is, of course, of great importance. With two rods in the boat the bow rod should cast over his left shoulder and the stern rod cast well to the right, working his flies across the water with the bob fly on the crest of the wavelets. Strike immediately on seeing or feeling a rise. The ratio of hooked fish to missed fish varies from day to day but I consider it good going to hook one in two.

If the fish being played jumps, lower the point of the rod sharply and

PETER ROSS

GREENWELL'S GLORY

TEAL & GREEN

BLACK PENNELL

BLACK & BLAE

BUTCHER

WOODCOCK & YELLOW

GROUSE & CLARET

WICKHAM'S FANCY

BLOODY BUTCHER

PARTRIDGE & YELLOW

Flies for Lake and Stillwater

if he runs under the boat plunge the rod deep into the water, taking care to keep the other flies on the cast well clear of the side of the boat; then bring your fish round to whichever end of the boat you are fishing, keeping the pressure on the fish with the tip of the rod as directly above him as possible.

All these points may be familiar to the experienced lake fisherman but they are probably worth mentioning for the benefit of those more used to other forms of angling.

With regard to flies, I personally like to fish with four flies on the cast. On most waters size fourteen is most usually fished in daytime with perhaps size sixteen if the water is very calm. When observing a rise on very calm water cast over the rise and leave the flies absolutely dead so as not to create any drag. At night, larger flies, preferably size twelve, produce good results.

I also always fish with double hooks. This has the effect of sinking the flies quicker if the fish are on the bottom, and improves the hooking percentage.

I suppose there are no two people who have the same preference for types of fly. Over the years we all come to have our favourites. Broadly speaking to have the following flies in my fly box gives me greater confidence and confidence is surely very much part of the fisherman's armoury. Some call it optimism.

Here are my favourites: Peter Ross, Greenwell's Glory, Teal and Green or Grouse and Green, Black Pennell or Black and Blae, Kingfisher Butcher, Woodcock and Yellow, Wickham's Fancy, Grouse and Claret, Priest, Bloody Butcher, and Partridge and Orange. The idea is to imitate the hatch on the water and attract the fish that way.

I invariably fish with a green and a black fly on each cast and having selected my flies do not generally do much chopping and changing after I have started fishing. I also often tie a large orange-coloured fly on a centre dropper. It attracts the fish and then they usually take one of the other flies.

Lake trout do not behave in the same way as river trout. The river trout have a permanent station, leaving it only to spawn and returning to the same station in the spring.

Lake trout cruise about over a wide area in their search for food, which they take in the form of plankton as well as many other forms of food. It is possible that the different depths at which the angler finds his fish from day to day are necessitated by the supply of plankton. The trout nearly always cruise against the wind and keep their heads to any current that there may be. In loch fishing it pays to advertise!

If one spots a rising fish one should cast four or five feet to the windward side as they move fairly rapidly. It is likely that they travel up and down the wind in a restricted elongated circle which varies according to the temperature and the depth of the water.

Trout are also gregarious. When they find a place where there is a rise of nymph or fly they collect together and confine themselves to short drifts. At that exciting moment when both rods hook a fish at the same time, it will be almost certain that, either by good luck or good judgement, you will have hit on such a spot.

There are, however, certain parts of a loch where trout will confine themselves to fixed stations such as the mouth of streams and burns. Burn mouths are therefore obvious places to try. On the other hand there are certain other likely places and signs to be looked for which will help in locating fish. I give a list of some of them in the hope that they will be helpful, particularly to the fisherman on a water he is not familiar with:

Streaks of foam. Trout cruise up channels of foam and seize the flies sticking to them.

Cast in front of weeds and rushes. They grow in a muddy bottom from which larvae emerge and rise to the surface and also support shrimp and fresh water snails.

Near rocks, sunken islands and promontories.

Along edges of banks where the shallow meets the deep. A change in the shades of water will help to locate these.

Along wooded shores and trees where caterpillars drop onto the water.

On shore on windy days in the foam and rough water. The flies are generally washing up onto the shore and I have hooked some very good fish within a few feet of the edge of the lake. I remember killing twenty-two fish on short drifts onto the shore on Ullswater one afternoon.

Edge of calm and ripple where the flies seem to lie.

Seagulls and swallows will be following the area of the lake where the flies are hatching. Watch them.

Move about the lake to find rising fish or shelter.

Wind plays an important part in fishing lakes, by casting with the breeze a team of wet flies from a boat which is drifting broadside on and before the wind. Of particular importance is what the wind carries with it; the trout will congregate where flies have been blown onto the water.

The wind will also change an area of still water from oily calmness to a gentle ruffle or roughness with waves and broken crests. We need a gentle breeze to quicken the surface of the water for wet fly fishing; on a calm day the boat will not drift and the fish will become most suspicious of any movement.

A rough idea of the depths of a lake helps considerably towards deciding on the most suitable method of angling. In deep waters we cannot expect a large and varied supply of insects. It would be a foolish trout indeed who would expend energy coming to the surface through two or three feet, or even more, to take any but large insects such as the Mayfly or Great Red Sedge. The use of ordinary flies in the sizes adapted to river fishing is therefore not recommended. When the lake is shallow, and where the bottom is covered with vegetation, there will be many insects which the trout can catch without wasting his energy, so the depth and character of the water are often indications of whether fish will come readily for a small fly, wet or dry, or need a team of large flies to attract them.

When I was a boy of seven I was taught to fish a lake by my uncle. He told me when making a cast one should stop the rod when it is pointing at the top of the surrounding mountains or hills and let the cast and line float down onto the water to avoid making any splash. Providing one is not too close under the hills I have always found this a very good tip indeed.

Another thing I have learned about fishing flies is that no matter what species they will not catch fish unless they are in the water!

The artificial nymph

The fishing for trout with the artificial nymph is the most recent of all fishing techniques to be recognised as a legitimate and separate sub-division of the fly fisherman's art.

Although the use of the nymph as a wet fly has long been experimented with, it was really the late G. E. M. Skues, who died in 1949, who first rationalised the principle and pioneered its development.

Nymphing has a restricted field in which it can be successfully used. It is essentially only effective on chalk streams where the water is clear and the feeding trout visible.

The advantage of using a nymph as opposed to a normal wet fly or in

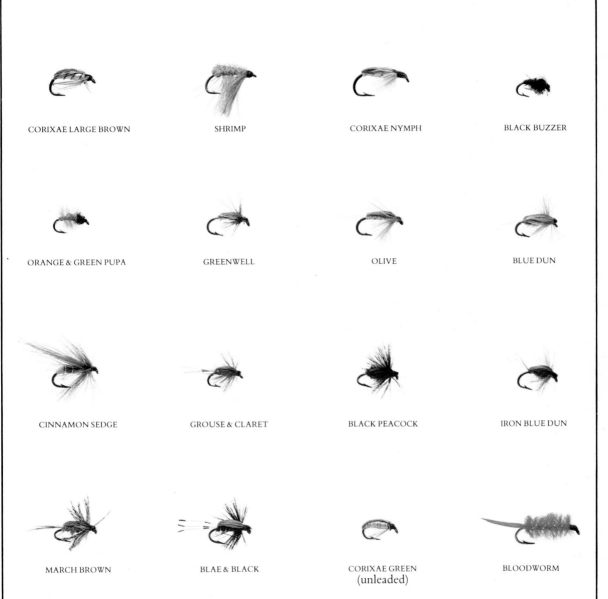

CORIXAE LARGE BROWN

SHRIMP

CORIXAE NYMPH

BLACK BUZZER

ORANGE & GREEN PUPA

GREENWELL

OLIVE

BLUE DUN

CINNAMON SEDGE

GROUSE & CLARET

BLACK PEACOCK

IRON BLUE DUN

MARCH BROWN

BLAE & BLACK

CORIXAE GREEN
(unleaded)

BLOODWORM

Artificial Nymphs

preference to a dry fly is that it makes possible attracting a fish feeding on the emerging fly hatching on the bottom of the river and rising to the surface to complete its transformation into a fully formed insect. In no way is it imitative of a drowning fly.

It is for this reason that the dressings in some cases are so light as to be what the late Oliver Kite described as the 'bare hook nymph'. The general conception in the tying of a nymph dressing is to use the hackle to stimulate the legs of the nymph. For successful operation, it is necessary to ensure that the nymph when put on the water should sink quickly. To achieve this the use of fine copper wire instead of the usual silk tying is an effective solution.

The technique of fishing the nymph is, having observed a feeding fish, to cast upstream well above it to allow time for the fly to sink by the time it comes into visual range; then by a slight tug of the line the nymph will appear to the trout to be rising from the river bed.

There are, of course, many patterns to be found on the market which do not precisely conform to the classic conception of the nymph, notably the Bloodworm and the Shrimp illustrated here.

These are included because, although not strictly nymphs, they are designed to be fished in precisely the same way.

To illustrate a greater number of nymphs would be repetitive as they are largely deviations of standard fly dressings. Of the flies illustrated the Greenwell, to me, typifies the animal.

Salmon flies of
North America

~

COL. JOSEPH D. BATES Jr.

Colonel Bates has written several books on fishing flies and fly fishing. He has collected thousands of antique and modern flies which are destined for permanent museum exhibition. A retired advertising agency executive, he served in the south-western Pacific during the Second World War and was retired from the Army of the United States after twenty-seven years' service. He and his wife Helen (also an angler) live in Longmeadow, Massachusetts.

The genesis of the Atlantic salmon fly seems to have been in England late in the fifteenth century when the ancient classic *The Treatyse of Fishing with an Angle*, attributed to a piscatorial nun named Juliana Berners, was published. In it she gave the dressings of twelve seasonal trout flies, several evidently having been used for salmon. In a few we recognise the ancestors of modern favourites, the March Brown, for instance. These were very simple patterns made from whatever was handy, such as wools and barnyard feathers, or feathers obtained by fowling.

While North America enjoyed no such ancient heritage, the birth of salmon flies there was quite similar with one drastic exception; wings ordinarily were of hair rather than of parts of feathers.

Whoever dressed the first North American salmon fly has become lost in obscurity. A reliable angling historian stated that he had seen a family Bible which belonged to a Newfoundland family named Stirling in which are handwritten entries dating between the years of 1720 and 1896. One of the entries, dated 1795, describes a hair-wing fly called the Red Cow fly and says that salmon were caught on it. The paucity of records of those days is because settlers in the Maritimes had little time to fish for fun. They were too busy eking out an existence in a relatively new country.

These early salmon flies evidently had descriptive names. When the originator of the Red Cow fly, for example, reported that he had hooked a whopper on it, everybody thereabouts knew that it had been tied from the hair of a Hereford he had brought from England and that it had a body dubbed from the underfur of the red cow and a wing of the guard hairs of the same animal.

Similarly, it was obvious to everybody that a Ten Bear fly had ten black bear hairs in its wing – that is, it was a sparsely dressed one. A Twenty Bear fly probably was considered rather overdressed, except for high water, and an Ordinary Bear fly was composed of a bunch of hairs whose number nobody had bothered to estimate, probably because the fishing was rather good at the time.

During the hundred or so years following these early beginnings newer materials made North American salmon flies more attractive but the wings of the most popular ones still usually are of hair; hair from squirrels (gray, fox, pine, red and black), bucktail (dyed in various colours), calf, fox, fitch and so forth. Later the gaudy, complicated classics from Britain were introduced, and they are still used to a declining extent. Many modern anglers spurn these fancy mixed or built-wing patterns as being unnecessary or too difficult to dress. Their beauty, however, is contagious, resulting in simplifications such as the substitution of dyed hair mixed in similar colours for wings.

Both hair-wing and feather-wing patterns still have their advocates. Those preferring hair-wings feel that they are easier to prepare, less prone to damage, and more particularly because the wings provide a more translucent appearance, pulsating in currents for more enticing action. They agree that the more opaque feather-wings are more attractive, but they won't give up much ground beyond that.

The translucent, pulsating advantages which can be made possible in the wings of salmon flies were not lost to some of the dressers in the British Isles. Michael Rogan, the great professional of Ballyshannon, made mixed-wing patterns choosing two or three fibres from each feather and then separating each fibre and rolling them all together until he got them absolutely mixed. Why didn't he use hair instead? Probably because he considered it rather vulgar! I once sat beside an old gentleman on a famous river and watched him with horror as he took a beautiful Jock Scott and carefully separated each fibre with a pin. Since he belonged to the club and I was a guest, I refrained from asking why he didn't use a hair-wing for the same effect.

It is fun to use the fancy flies that catch fishermen but it seems more practical to most of us North Americans to favour simpler patterns which have proved their superior ability to hook fish.

My new book *Atlantic Salmon Flies & Fishing* (Scribner & Sons, New

York) gives detailed dressings for over one hundred North American salmon flies. Of these about two-thirds are hair-wings, including nearly all of the most modern popular ones. Most are now superfluous but are given for fly-dressers and because of historic interest. I would be content with less than half a dozen in several sizes; the Rusty, Blue and Silver Rats, Cosseboom, and a black one with a fluorescent butt. We actually need very few patterns, including bright, medium and dark, selected with regard to whether or not the salmon are facing the sun, whether the day is dark or bright, and/or the degree of clarity of the water. Having said this, brother anglers will comment that I don't practise what I preach. I habitually carry several boxes containing hundreds. Unnecessary fly patterns, taken along 'just in case', are part of the fun of fishing!

North American anglers, many of whom are fly-dressers, like to vary the patterns they use, based on standard ones. A type that is currently very popular is predominantly black or very dark with fluorescent floss at its tail. This may be as a butt or as the rear part of the body. Colours don't seem to matter much, but green, red or yellow vie in popularity. A small amount of fluorescence is more effective than too much.

Taking salmon on the dry fly is a North American development which, after more than half a century, remains pretty much so because anglers in other countries around the North Atlantic think, rightly or wrongly, that the method is ineffective there. Some give colder water temperatures as the reason, perhaps resulting in fewer insects on the streams, but we could venture the opinion that the more logical reason is lack of practice or of experience. In any event, anglers who have fly-fished for most game species in both fresh and salt water usually consider that hooking an Atlantic salmon on a dry fly is the supreme peak of angling thrills.

One of the first men to do it was Colonel Ambrose Monell, on New Brunswick's Upsalquitch before the outbreak of the First World War. His companion on many angling expeditions, George M. L. La Branche, describes it in his *The Salmon and the Dry Fly* (Houghton Mifflin Company, Boston and New York, 1924), a classic which has been reprinted:

> 'Believing as I did, that salmon do not feed in fresh water, I hesitated to introduce the subject of fishing for them with a floating fly. Divining, perhaps, what was in my mind, my friend (Colonel Monell) calmly announced that he had killed a fifteen-pound salmon two years before on a dry fly, and assured me that it was not an accident. He had seen the fish rising and, having failed to interest it with any of the wet flies in his box, he

had deliberately cast across the upstream with a number 12 'Whirling Dun', floating it down over the fish, which took it at once. It was the taking of this fish, and the rising of six or seven others which he did not hook, that convinced him it would be possible to kill fish with the dry fly when the water was low.'

Mr La Branche goes on to recount other salmon taken on dry flies during this trip and others. Since those early days hooking salmon on dry flies has become standard practice in North America; in fact, they can often become interested in floaters when they won't look at anything else.

In other countries the fact that salmon haven't been taken on dry flies doesn't mean that it can't be done. It was said that it couldn't be done in Iceland, but several of us have done it too often for it to have been an accident. We have done it in pools and runs after the fish had refused conventional wet flies. I haven't tried it in the United Kingdom and other countries mainly due to conditions existing when I was there, but it could be 'an ace in the hole' when other methods have failed.

We need few dry fly patterns, but we need them in several sizes, from very large to quite small. My vote would be for three of Lee Wulff's famous innovations; dark or black, medium, and light or bright. My favourite, however, is the Bomber, a monstrosity that might evoke shudders from purists. This has an oval-shaped body of spun and closely clipped deer body hair (black, grey, brown, or white) with a ribbing of a large hackle in contrasting colour wound through it. It has a tail of the former material and a 'wing' of the same tied in to extend forward at an angle of about forty-five degrees. It is difficult to sink but, if it does so, can be retrieved wet – often with good results. While flies of this type usually are drifted without drag, they often can be very effective when skittered.

As in other countries, North Americans often have low-water problems with dour or 'reluctant' salmon. We know of no sure ways to hook them, but we know of several that can be tried. One is by methods just mentioned. Another is to show them 'something very different', either in pattern or method of presentation, or both. Before commenting on this let us remember why we think salmon take flies when we know they don't need feed in fresh water. I may differ with some by insisting that there are only two very different reasons; curiosity and anger. The first is indicated by a 'pluck' or casual take. The second normally results in a slashing strike. The first is remindful of a baby seeing a small nearby object. Curiosity gives it the instinct to put it in its mouth. The second is caused by defence of territory. Salmon stake a claim to a good lie and try to defend it from other fish or anything else that encroaches. A salmon with the latter instinct may let an ordinary fly drift by without objection, but it may strike savagely at an object (usually larger) that indicates even a small threat of invasion.

Experience indicates that these two instincts can be handled in a similar manner, if they can be handled at all. We, on this side of the Atlantic, feel it expedient to let the 'something very different' be a large and long 'bucktail'; the type of 'fly' that simulates a baitfish, rather than something with more of the shape of an insect (which normal salmon flies are supposed to represent). Such a bucktail (or streamer fly) would be fished actively, as a baitfish swims. It would be slim, and about three inches long. Colours (again) depend on the fishing conditions previously mentioned, but this may make little or no difference; a pattern predominantly black, one very bright, and a medium one, such as mostly grey. The bright one can be most effective; a long silver or gold body with a longer wing of yellow and red, such as yellow over red over yellow, or brown over yellow. The object is to fish this in as many unusual ways (at the salmon's level) as can be devised, usually with plenty of action. Dour salmon are difficult to entice, but there often are one or two which will succumb to such temptation!

BUTTERFLY
(also called Ingalls' Butterfly and Ingalls' Splay-wing Coachman)
Head colour: Black.
Tail: A dozen or so fibres of a bright red hackle, fairly long.
Body: Wound with rusty peacock herl (some instructions say that one turn of herl is added in front of the wing, but the original pattern does not show this; (the body originally was tied with black wool but Mr Ingalls later preferred the peacock).
Wing: A divided wing of white goat hair, slightly longer than the body and set a bit above the body, slanted backwards at an angle of about 45°. The wings are very sparse and the hair should be from a small goat, as the hair from large goats is too brittle and too stiff.
Hackle: Two turns of a brown hackle wound on as a collar, one turn behind the wings and one in front. The hackle is about half as long as the wing hair, is applied dry-fly style, and should be very sparse.

BLACK BEAR
Head colour: Black.
Tail: Two thin sections of a black feather, such as dyed swan or goose.
Body: Black wool.

Throat: A small bunch of black bear hair, extending to end of hook.
Wing: A small bunch of black bear hair, extending to end of tail.

MUDDLER MINNOW
Head colour: Black.
Tail: Two narrow sections of natural (light mottled) turkey wing quill, of moderate length.
Body: Flat gold tinsel; tied in about a quarter of an inch behind eye; wound to tail and back to starting point.
Rest of dressing:
1   Apply a small bunch of grey squirrel hairs as a wing, tied on about a quarter of an inch behind hook eye, extending two thirds length of hook shank.
2   On each side of the hair tie in a section of dark mottled turkey wing about a quarter of an inch wide, extending to tail (sections from a right and a left quill feather).
3   Apply over this a bunch of about 75 to 100 deer body hairs (as much as half the thickness of a lead pencil), leaving about a quarter of an inch of the hair in front of the thread. Take three or four turns to secure and pull tight until hairs start to flare out and spread lightly around the bend of the hook.
4   Cut another bunch of deer hair and, after securing as above, cut off rear part so about a quarter of an inch is in front and behind the thread. Pull tight to make the hair flare out as in 3.
5   Clip the flared short hair to desired shape, usually in cone shape towards eye of hook. Also clip off and trim to the desired shape about half the bunch of hairs applied in 3, leaving enough to complete the desired dressing of the wing (the remainder of clipped hair adding to the dressing of the collar).

RUSTY RAT
Tag: Oval gold tinsel.
Tail: Three or four peacock sword fibres, tied in rather short.
Body: Rear half: bright yellow floss, forward half: peacock herl. A length of the yellow floss extends as a veiling from the middle of the body nearly to the end of the body on top of the fly.
Ribbing: Oval gold tinsel.
Wing: A small bunch of the guard hairs of a grey fox.
Hackle: A grizzly hackle tied on as a collar.
Cheeks: Jungle cock (optional).

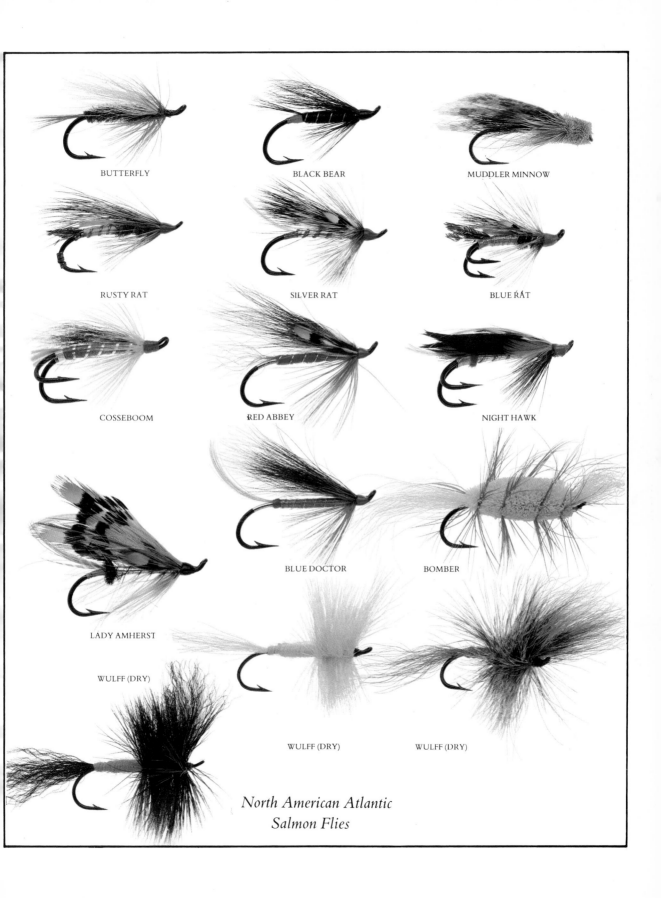

BUTTERFLY

BLACK BEAR

MUDDLER MINNOW

RUSTY RAT

SILVER RAT

BLUE RAT

COSSEBOOM

RED ABBEY

NIGHT HAWK

LADY AMHERST

BLUE DOCTOR

BOMBER

WULFF (DRY)

WULFF (DRY)

WULFF (DRY)

North American Atlantic
Salmon Flies

SILVER RAT

a variation of the Grey Rat, which is dressed as follows:
Tag: A few turns of flat gold tinsel (use oval gold tinsel on double hooks).
Tail: A very small golden pheasant crest feather.
Body: Under-fur of grey fox, spun on.
Ribbing: Flat gold tinsel.
Wing: A small bunch of the guard hairs of a grey fox.
Hackle: A grizzly hackle tied on as a collar.
Cheeks: Jungle cock, short (optional).

In the Silver Rat, the body is dressed with silver tinsel, with oval gold ribbing (remember to use red tying thread on this and all other flies in the series).

COSSEBOOM

Head colour: Red.
Tag: Silver tinsel.
Tail: A small golden pheasant crest feather.
Body: Orange silk floss.
Ribbing: Flat silver tinsel.
Wing: Extremely small bunches of four items: bronze peacock herl over which is grey quirrel over which is green peacock herl over which is fox squirrel. All four are repeated over this to make eight tiny bunches, one on top of the other.
Hackle: A black and white teal feather, wound on as a collar.
Cheeks: A very small teal body feather, one on each side, over which are short jungle cock eyes, if available.

RED ABBEY

Head colour: Black or red.
Tag: Flat embossed or oval silver tinsel.
Tail: A small section of the wing of red ibis, swan, or goose, or a very small bunch of red bucktail.
Body: Red silk floss, or wool.
Ribbing: Flat embossed or oval silver tinsel.
Throat: A few turns of a brown hackle applied as a collar, pulled down and tied back slightly.
Wing: A small bunch of light brown squirrel tail hairs or brown bucktail.
Cheeks: Jungle cock (optional).

NIGHT HAWK
Head colour: Red.
Tag: Oval silver tinsel.
Tip: Yellow silk floss.
Tail: A golden pheasant crest feather, over which is a very small strand or two of blue kingfisher, half as long as the crest feather.
Butt: Two or three turns of red wool.
Body: Flat silver tinsel.
Ribbing: Oval silver tinsel.
Wing: Two sections of black turkey feather, extending to the tip of the tail.
Throat: A small bunch of black hackle fibres, rather short.
Shoulders: Jungle cock, half as long as the wing.
Cheeks: Sections of a blue kingfisher feather, set outside and over the jungle cock, nearly as long as the jungle cock but narrow enough so as not to conceal it.
Topping: A golden pheasant crest feather, curving to the end of the tail.

LADY AMHERST
Thread: Black.
Tag: Fine oval silver tinsel or wire and golden yellow floss.
Tail: A topping and strands of teal.
Butt: Black ostrich herl.
Body: Flat silver tinsel.
Ribbing: Oval silver tinsel.
Hackle: Badger, from butt, sparse.
Wings: Two jungle cock feathers back to back extending to end of tail, veiled with two square-ended Amherst pheasant tippets on each side, the inner bars of which lie over the butt. Over these are two shorter round-ended Amherst pheasant tippets extending to the inner bars of the longer tippets so the outer black bars of the shorter feathers cover the inner black bars of the longer feathers (as in Ranger patterns).
Sides: Jungle cock.
Cheeks: Blue chatterer (kingfisher).
Topping: A golden pheasant crest feather.
Horns: Blue and yellow macaw.
Head: Black thread.

This famous classic-style North American pattern was originated about 1925 by George D. B. Bonbright, president of the Seaboard Airline

Railway, and was extensively used by him on Canadian rivers; especially the Grand Cascapedia. The fly is still so popular there that it is the only one guides usually want anglers to use; normally in sizes as large as 5/0 for that big river.

BLUE DOCTOR
Head colour: Red.
Tag: Oval silver tinsel.
Tail: A golden pheasant crest feather.
Butt: Bright red silk floss.
Body: Light blue silk floss, dressed thin.
Ribbing: Oval silver tinsel.
Throat: A light blue hackle applied as a collar and tied back slightly; fairly long.
Wing: A small bunch of grey squirrel hair.

BOMBER
Head colour: Use any appropriately coloured head.
Tail: A fairly large and rather short bunch of the same deer body hair that will be used for the body of the fly (other materials are often used, such as calf, woodchuck, etc).
Wing: A fairly short bunch of the same body hair tied so as to extend forward at an angle of about 45° (this forward and upward bunch of hair is called a wing for want of a better term; the upward slant keeps it free of the eye of the hook).
Body: Natural deer hair (grey, brown, and white are regularly used) spun on, tightly massed, flared out and clipped to a smooth cigar shape, tapering towards the tail and slightly towards the head. The body should be clipped so that about one third is below the hook shank and two thirds above it to allow plenty of clearance between body and barb. To produce a dense body, rather small bunches of body hair should be used. Many anglers like the body rather roughly clipped.
Ribbing: A large brown hackle (or one of any other desired colour) tied in at the tail and palmered through the clipped body from tail to head.

GREY WULFF
Tail: Natural brown bucktail.
Body: Blue-grey wool.
Wings: Natural brown bucktail.
Hackle: Two blue-grey saddle hackles.

WHITE WULFF

Tail: White bucktail.
Body: Cream-coloured wool.
Wings: White bucktail.
Hackle: Two light badger hackles.

ROYAL WULFF

Tail: White bucktail.
Body: Rear and front quarters are butted with peacock herl: middle half is scarlet wool or silk.
Wings: White bucktail.
Hackle: Two brown saddle hackles.

Appendix

Hook sizes

The following illustration is given as a guide to hook sizes although it should be noted that sizes vary very slightly from manufacturer to manufacturer.

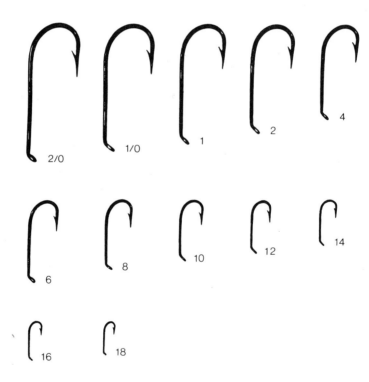

Index

Numbers in italics refer to illustrations